D1610086

Good Morning, Brothers!
Jack Dash

THE AUTHOR AT HOME   *Edward Hayes*

Good Morning, Brothers!

Jack Dash

1969
LAWRENCE & WISHART
LONDON

PRINTED IN GREAT BRITAIN
BY UNWIN BROTHERS LIMITED
WOKING AND LONDON

Acknowledgment

When I first discussed this book with Lawrence & Wishart Ltd., I explained that I'd never written a book before and perhaps lacked the kind of skills that authors require. They said not to worry, just write it as it comes and they would find someone to see that it had the right number of full-stops, commas and paragraphs.

So I didn't worry. I sat down at my kitchen table and wrote just as it came, on big ruled pages with a thick felt pen. The fact that it has become a book is due to the hard slog put in over many weeks of her spare time by Nan Green, to whom I am accordingly grateful.

Contents

I

Boyhood

"Dad!"

"Yes, son?"

"It was Empire Day today at school. We all marched out into the playground, and each class had a Union Jack at the front. Some of the boys wore their Scout uniforms, Dad, and in the middle of the playground there was a platform and one of the girls was dressed up as Britannia, with a girl each side of her in Girl Guide uniform. We all stood to attention while the Scouts played their bugles. Then the headmaster told us all about the Empire, and how it was built by our forefathers and King George was a sort of father to all the people in the colonies, and before we came to those countries they were all savages and the kids had no boots and no schools, and they didn't know about God either. He said they're still poor but they're a lot happier now. That's good, isn't it?"

"It certainly is, son. Now I want you to get some errands for me, and then you can go out and play in the street."

I stood waiting for the money. Suddenly I burst out:

"Dad, when are you going to get *me* some boots?"

Poor Dad, he looked so helpless. It was the first time I had known him to be stuck for words. However, he told me how sorry he was, but I must be patient a bit longer because he couldn't get any work. He was going to see a man called the Relieving Officer, who would give him some tickets for food, and he would see if he could get a ticket for some boots for me.

There were to be many incidents like this in my school days. As I grew older I heard neighbours speak of "going round to the Bun House"—the expression they used for the parish charity house, the Board of Guardians for the relief of the poor. The unfortunate ones would be secretive about it. It hurt their pride and made them feel humiliated, though the circumstances were not of their own making. Later, as a result of the struggles of the labour movement, relief tickets were done away with and money was issued instead. After that there was no need to creep furtively into the butchers' and grocers' shops, trying to avoid a neighbour.

I first saw the light of day in a maternity hospital in the Metropolitan Borough of Southwark, south of the Thames. I lived and played through my boyhood in Rockingham Street, a side street off a traffic junction and shopping centre near the Elephant and Castle, the famous pub whose name, so they say, is a corruption of *Infanta of Castile*. My mother, whose Christian names were Rose Gertrude and single name Johns, died when she was only forty years old. I was seven at the time of her death. She died of consumption—the term T.B. was not common in those days, and the disease was very often fatal.

Of the years before her death I have very little recollection. But my brothers, who cared for me as the baby of the family, adored her memory and would sit on our street doorstep and tell me stories about her until I fell asleep. Apparently she came of a somewhat snobbish middle-class family of the Victorian period who owned a working-class tenement, known as the Haberdashers' Estate, in the north London Borough of Hoxton. Hoxton, with its open market and the tough but lovable costermongers who were familiar figures of all London street markets in those days, was a pretty rough neighbourhood with a notorious area known as "The Nile", where the police patrolled in pairs for safety. The name Haberdashers had no connection with my mother's family. Indeed, they would have considered it an insult if anyone had had the audacity to suggest such a thing. They were of Welsh stock and West Country origin.

Mother's career before her marriage was on the stage. She was a professional actress playing in drama, and that is how she met my father, who was a general stage-hand, scene-shifter and property man. They fell in love and married. This was regarded as a great blow by the Johns family, who considered that their daughter had married out of her class. They disowned her.

My parents were very happy with each other, but they fell on hard times. Dad lost his job and could find no other work. They went through periods of extreme poverty. More than once, my brothers told me, they came home from school and found mother sitting on an upturned bucket, quietly sobbing, and every stick of furniture taken by the bailiffs. Happily, the Johns family was eventually moved and they remembered some of their Christian morals. They offered Dad a job as a rent collector on their Hoxton estate. They thought that since he was a big man and a teetotaller, he would be ideal for the job. For a period everything went along fine; the family was eating regularly and building a new home, and Mother was very happy. But there was a snag in the environment. Dad was an extremely talented musician, a good sport and a great one for telling humorous stories. He was what you would call a character, and very popular with the tenants. They would often invite him to weekend parties, and gradually he took to drinking. This was the beginning of the end for us, and eventually broke our family life. Often he would allow tenants to keep back their rent in order to hold a week-end party, to which he would be invited for his gifts as an entertainer. On the following Monday he would tell some plausible tale to the estate office about the Smiths or the Joneses being down on their luck, how there was unemployment in this family and the head of that one had broken his leg and couldn't pay the rent.

Like all good things, this came to an end. The truth was discovered through neighbours' gossip and petty jealousy. Dad was hauled before his employers and summarily sacked. The ties with my mother's family were broken and the break-up began. Dad could not get another job anywhere, not even casual work. Poor Mother took to cleaning public-house bar-rooms to help feed us and keep a roof over our heads. What with undernourishment and the long hours of scrubbing filthy floors, she fell ill. The harrowing experience of doing "moonlight flits" to escape from arrears of rent, and eviction into the street when no moonlight flit was possible, finally wore her out, and she died during World War One.

Poor Mother. What tremendous efforts she made to keep us together and feed us. My brothers told me that on many occasions she had walked the streets with me in her arms, singing for a few coppers to buy food. Once, to prevent her children being taken away following an eviction, she had taken us all to the park for several days, and at night the commissionaire of the Canterbury Theatre, who knew her from her acting days, had let us sleep in the stalls after the last performance. But the management got to know and that kindness came to an end.

Mother's death was a tremendous shock to the old man. He gave up heavy drinking, and for a while things began to look up. My two older brothers at home were working; the third, the eldest, was a regular soldier serving twenty-one years in a famous Irish regiment, the Connaught Rangers, and was sending money home. Again we were eating regular meals.

But the brief post-war boom had ended in 1921, unemployment was rapidly increasing, while the employers openly attacked the trade unions and insisted on lengthening hours. Dad and my brothers were all out of a job. Hunger hit the family once more. I was a growing lad, and my brothers could not take me on their knees and sing me to sleep as they had done in previous hard times.

The old man, in spite of his many weaknesses, was basically a good man, and he endeavoured for the rest of his life to atone for the past, but the cards were stacked against him. With unemployment and failing health, he had no chance. But he did his best to keep us from want. He would beg, steal, borrow—you name it and he would try it, owing money everywhere, his credit exhausted in the local shops. Many's the time I have heard him say: "I've got to wait until it's dark before I can go out, I owe so much to so many folk."

Eventually Dad died, of a lung complaint he had contracted during the 1914–18 war. He was seeking work, collapsed in the streets, was picked up by an ambulance and taken to hospital, and died undergoing oxygen treatment. We were so poor; to have paid life insurance in those days was impossible. As in countless other working-class families, the first demand on any money we were fortunate enough to obtain was rent and food.

Dad was buried by the Parish. His coffin was conveyed from the hospital to the cemetery in a vehicle known as "the Rattler". For the mourners, one coach was provided by the authorities. In our case, there were more mourners than the coach would hold, so Uncle Albert, Dad's youngest brother, had to make his way to the cemetery by tramcar.

There is often a streak of comedy in the midst of life's tragedies. Uncle Albert, unemployed like the rest, only had sufficient money for the single fare. When the problem was explained, the foreman undertaker kindly allowed him to ride back standing on the rear axle of the coach. The kids were just coming out of school as we made the return journey. In those days of horse-drawn vehicles it was the kids' custom, if they saw a smart lad trying to snatch a ride on the back of a cab or a cart, to yell: "Whip behind, guvnor!" to the driver, and over would come the whip with a swish. That's what happened to Uncle Albert. The coachman had forgotten about the arrangement, and caught him a real slash in the face. If the old man had been able to witness it, he would have had a good laugh.

Without doubt the old man was a great character, a product of his generation and time. Full of humour and an excellent story-teller, he would make friends within a few moments of acquaintance. His philosophy of life, though he never used that phrase, was: you only pass this way once, so enjoy it—but don't hurt people in doing so; if you can't make money, make friends— if you can't get on with people, then there is something wrong with you. I've tried to follow him in this. To this day when I meet new acquaintances, I always try to find the things we can agree on. The rest will follow with time. I have made countless friends, some of them in quite exalted strata of society, but I have always proclaimed my membership of the Communist Party and my aim to help build a communist society.

One closing anecdote about my father trying to atone for his past: on occasions when we were without food (which was more often than not) he would put on a large overcoat with no lining to the pockets and go out on a "shopping expedition". He wasn't a religious man, but he would look at me and say: "Ah well, the Lord knows who needs it most, let's hope He ain't forgotten us." Very late in the evening he would return and load the kitchen table with all sorts of food, saying: "The Lord helps those who help themselves." I used to think he was a magician. Once he got a job as prop and baggage man at the old Elephant and Castle Theatre, and one Saturday night—I always waited up for him, for I loved to hear him tell about the music-hall turns—he produced from out of his magic overcoat a beautiful white Angora rabbit. It was one of those rabbits that is produced out of a conjuror's top hat, and then it would jump over the conjuror's wand. Our old man, with his sense of the theatre, held the broomstick in front of bunny, who dutifully jumped over—not into a top hat but into a big saucepan, and fed the family for a couple of days!

Before leaving my boyhood memories I must pay tribute to the working-class mothers of Rockingham Street, Southwark, where I grew up as an orphan. There was always a welcome for me at their kitchen tables, regardless of how little they had themselves. I specially remember wonderful, kind Mrs Boyce, mother of fourteen kids, who would send them out to look for me, and if it wasn't a dinner she would shove a large, thick slice of bread and treacle into my hand, saying in her gentle voice: "There, get that down yer. I wish it could be more."

What a wonderful community spirit existed in those years between the two world wars, and what terrific pride the women took in their homes. On Saturday mornings, out would come Mum or daughter with a steamy pail of soapy water and a scrubbing brush. Down they would go on their knees and scrub not only the doorstep but the pavement outside the street door right out to the curb. The knocker and doorhandle glowed with polish and to walk into the kitchen—well, though it might be sparsely furnished it had an air of luxury, that kitchen table with its embroidered cloth spread out all neat and even. The stove and fireplace with fender and tongs would shine so black you could see your face in them. The kettle, also shining black, would be steaming away on it, and above would be the mantelpiece, with vases and a clock, and a family portrait on the wall above that. The whole kitchen would instantly convey to you the loving care and pride of the family in their home.

At Easter, especially on Good Friday, communal skipping would take place. Whole families would be out in the road, with the men turning the skipping-rope for the children. Even the Mums and daughters took part in the skipping games. In the evening the parents would go off to the "local" for a drink. The women would gossip while the men would be playing darts, shove-halfpenny, dominoes or cribbage. At closing time they would go back home for a ding-dong, or a "knees-up" as it was called in those days. Most families had someone who was a bit of a musician and could play the "old Joanna" (the piano), the accordion or the mouth-organ. Each gave his or her favourite song in turn. This communal spirit carried on right throughout the years of the second world war, especially during the London blitz.

Wherever I travelled as a boy I always met sympathy and help. I am certain that it was this experience that helped shape my character. Somewhere in my subconscious, I think, there exists the feeling that in doing what I have done or will continue to do in the class struggle, I am returning the kindness shown me by those working-class mothers who, though they had large families of their own to feed and clothe, would always find an extra something for me. This, I have no doubt, is typical of working-class mothers the world over.

I recall how we Cockney kids would scheme sometimes to obtain a few coppers for a meal. Our group would set off to walk to Hyde Park; it was our countryside. It was a long walk for us kids, badly shod or with no footwear at all. After skylarking around, perhaps having a swim in the Serpentine, we would be ravenous, dead tired and none too eager for the long trek home. One of our lads, Charlie by name, had a glass eye. He would take this out and give it one of us to keep in our pockets. Then we would draw near to one of the places where the old dears used to sit in their deck-chairs, sunning themselves and renewing the tan left over from their holidays. Charlie would begin to sob loudly. It never failed. One of the old dears was sure to enquire what was wrong. The weeping Charlie, at his Oscar best, would tell them that he had lost his eye and describe the awful walloping he would get when he arrived home. The kind old dears would open their handbags . . . we were very polite and thankful to them. With our arms round poor Charlie we would make our way out of the Park—hop onto a bus and, once arrived at the Elephant and Castle, go to the nearest coffee-shop and have a good blow-out: a pair of kippers, two thick slices and a large tea. Charlie would pay the bill, and if there was any money left over—if!—then that was his. What a feast!—it was like Belshazzar's feast to us.

No doubt about it. Poverty sharpened our wits and our resourcefulness. And this was to be an asset to us when we entered the adult world of no quarter, every man for himself—until we hit the organised labour movement of the trade unions and began to learn the real meaning of brotherhood.

2

Higher Education

I am now fourteen years old, school-leaving age, having been taught the three Rs, reading, writing and arithmetic, the basic elementary curriculum, and about to enter the toughest University of all—the University of Life. My college—the College of Industry.

The only talent with which Nature had endowed me was an ability to draw. My brother Frank, the second eldest, had taken on the responsibility of my care and upbringing. He suggested that I should seek an apprenticeship with an engraving firm. One was found—a small firm—and I was given a trial period before the apprenticeship papers were signed. However, the apprenticeship never materialised. Unemployment caught up with us, and we went back to Square One. My brother was one of the victims of the mass layoffs, so it was decided that I should look for an unskilled job; an apprentice's money was not enough to keep me.

So I left a skilled trade, to become a page-boy for J. Lyons of Cadby Hall, the Corner House and teashop king. I started as a page-boy on the opening night of the Coventry Street Corner House. It was the day West Ham lost the first Wembley Cup Final to Bolton Wanderers, if my memory serves me correctly. Both teams celebrated there.

My job was to stand by the cash-desk and copy into a notebook the number of each customer's bill. The numbers were given to me by the "Nippies" (waitresses) who were serving the various tables, and as the customer came to pay at the desk, I was to check his number and cross it off. If the customer attempted to pass me, I had to remind him that he had not paid. The poor Nippies were worried out of their lives lest a bill should get through, particularly if it happened to be a large one—for it would mean a deduction in their meagre pay.

Every day before going on duty, we page-boys would have to line up before the chief hall-porter in charge of the uniformed staff. These chaps were usually ex-members of the Regular Army who had spent twenty years of their lives Yes, Sir-ing and No, Sir-ing, and earning promotion by making sure that those beneath them did the same. Each morning we lined up in two open ranks; the chief hall-porter would strut around us like a Regimental Sergeant-Major, all beribboned and very pompous, inspecting our faces and hands, our shoes and our white gloves. He would talk about vigilance, and tell us that if a customer who was dining alone walked past us saying he was going to the toilet we must take a quick glance at his table to see if he had left something there that he would need to come back and fetch; if not, we were to make sure he paid his bill. Then he would dismiss us. He loved every moment of it.

I didn't last long with Joe Lyons. I got sacked because, while I was watching the hands of the resident violinist and listening to the beautiful music he was playing, two big bills were able to slip past the cash desk and through the swing doors. The poor "Nippy" almost fainted. Next day I was hauled before the staff manager and sacked on the spot.

Within ten minutes I had handed in my page-boy's uniform and received my cards and money. I wasn't even allowed to have the meal that was due to me.

I was scared to go home and break the news. Walking through the City I managed to find a new job, as office boy and messenger to an American firm called Elliot and Fisher, manufacturers of typewriter and accounting machines. I stayed with them for about two years, until a new managing director arrived on the scene, full of wonderful ideas for organisation and efficiency. As I have learned since, the moment you hear talk of organisation and efficiency someone is for the sack, for any employer who wants to change the working practices of his employees is not doing it for their benefit or that of his customers, the guiding principle for increased profits being governed by how low you keep your labour costs. So out went Jack, back again to Square One—unemployment.

My brother Frank was then regularly employed by a firm called Billings, wholesale book and periodical distributors, situated in a side turning off Ludgate Hill. He spoke for me and I was taken on as a "barrow-boy" whose job it was to haul a barrow loaded

B

with books and periodicals to different bookshops round the City and West End, with another lad making a team of two to a barrow. There was three teams in all, and it was very hard work, but being teenage lads we thoroughly enjoyed it, especially in the summer. Stripped to the waist, we used to compete as to which team could pull the heaviest load in the fastest time.

The guv'nor loved it. We were too young and naive to know why—until one day my brother Frank called us together and informed us that we were about to become a Union shop and we would have to join the Union, which we did. Then Frank gave us a short, simple talk on the meaning of trade unionism, and showed us how our team-competition aided nobody but the boss because it enabled him to employ a skeleton staff of cheap labour. Although we were all youngsters, we were sensible enough to listen to adult advice, and within two weeks the employer was forced to take on two extra lads and offer a bonus for any extra loads done. This was my first lesson in organised unity, which was to stay with me for the rest of my industrial life.

A few months later, the General Strike broke out. I was still a teenager in May 1926, and witnessed scenes of class-hatred and class solidarity that are deeply embedded in my memory and have never left me to this day. I recall that it was a Sunday, early evening, and there had been mass demonstrations in every London borough. I was at the Elephant and Castle in Southwark, and caught up with the terrific excitement of the crowd. Suddenly everyone was shouting abuse (it made the language of Lady Chatterley sound like a choir chant by comparison). All eyes were turned in one direction. Coming in from the direction of Westminster were car-loads of Special Reserves, all steel-helmeted with truncheons at the ready, the trucks protected with a kind of wire cage over the top to protect them from missiles aimed by the strikers. They were followed by Mounted Police, escorting a General omnibus with passengers, driven by a university student. (The historians tell us that the greater part of the strike-breakers came from the universities. I am quite confident that this would not happen today among the present generation of university students—they would be demonstrating alongside the strikers!)

Stones began to rain down from the tops of the adjacent tenement buildings onto the armoured vehicles. The mounted reserves and police were unseated from their horses. Running fights took place with the foot police. The bus was halted, the passengers were dragged out, a great crowd of men overturned the vehicle, which caught fire and began to blaze away. There were casualties everywhere. No quarter was given. Eventually reinforcements arrived and the police, Special Constables and Army Reserve men regained control.

On the Monday morning tanks and armoured cars were stationed outside the Bank of England and the Royal Exchange, manned by Scottish and Irish troops. Oh the cunning of the ruling class!—Northern troops in the south and Southern troops in the north! But as the strike continued the workers became more disciplined, more determined and better organised. The more vicious the methods used by the Establishment to smash the strike, the more clear the struggle became to every worker. It was they who were the creators of the nation's wealth and progress, and the time had come for a change in the order of things. In all the major towns and cities Workers' Councils were formed; there was one for each London borough, and no motor, tram, train or horse-drawn vehicle could move from one borough to another without a pass signed by the Workers' Councils—their authority was absolute.

The very few blacklegs got short shrift. Down at the docks, London's waterfront, any would-be scab would have been thrown into the dock. I recall, just a few years back, as I stood talking to an elderly docker, nodding a "Good morning" to another older chap as he passed. "Jack," said my old pal, "for Christ's sake don't lower yourself to talk to that no-good, dirty, black-legging, scabbing bastard!" Apparently he had scabbed in the big strike of 1912—and this was 1964!

The General Strike lasted nine days. Although there were more workers out on the ninth day, firmly united and determined to win, along came the sell-out. J. H. Thomas and the others were desperately afraid that the strike would become a real political challenge to the government, and they were determined that this should not happen. The T.U.C. called off the strike. This has become the principal policy of social-democracy the world over: in every crisis the workers are sold out and the capitalist class is left firmly entrenched with huge profits and power.

Back at the firm of Billings, some employees were not re-engaged and I was one of them. After many weeks of unemployment my pal, who had been sacked with me, convinced me that

it was better to join the Regular Army with bed and board, 2s. 9d.
a day, see the world and be a man's man. Monday morning, and
off we go to the nearest recruiting office. It was at Camberwell
Green. The Colour Sergeant Major welcomed us with open arms
and a big smile. What a kind man! For once our Cockney shrewdness deserted us. We were well and truly "conned". Little did we
know that he received a shilling for every recruit he swore in.
Lovely chap, he even went out of his way to make the intelligence
test easy. All we had to do was take down a bit of dictation given
by him at double-slow speed. I remember it yet: "The boy sat on
the doorstep with a broom in his hand. . . ."

Unfortunately my pal, who was a very good athlete, was a very
poor scholar. The sergeant could see that he was fidgety and
kept nudging me; in order not to lose that shilling commission,
the nice, kind understanding Sergeant left the room, knowing
full well what would happen. It did. I wrote two dictations and
we were both enlisted.

By this time I'd got some of my wits back, and in spite of his
"conning" to get us to join a regiment that required seven years
with the Colours and five with the Reserve, I wouldn't sign.
The crafty Sergeant could see his commission slipping from his
grasp. He quickly found an alternative—the Royal Army Service
Corps, horse transport, two years with the Colours and ten with
the Reserve. Apart from the two years and ten, the mere mention
of horse had me going. I am a great lover of animals, horses and
dogs in particular. I was sold, hook, line and sinker, and my pal
Charlie too.

Our training depot was at Woolwich Barracks, not far from
home. How enthusiastic and important we felt to get into our
uniforms and go home to show off, with dreams of captivating all
the girls.

The fashion then among serving men (perhaps it still continues)
was to get yourself tattooed. So on our first weekend passs we
visited the famous Burchett, whose shop was situated alongside
the Union Jack Hotel for servicemen. He must have tattooed
half the British Army in his lifetime. Anyhow, I chose "I love
Nell"; this was the name of the girl I was courting, who later
became my wife and comrade throughout my life. (The finest
decision I have made.) Charlie was more grandiose in his choice;
he was tattooed with a dagger piercing a heart with the words
"Death Before Dishonour" on a scroll twisted round a snake.

Five weeks later Charlie went on the run, blew off the side, deserted. I have never seen him since.

However, I soldiered on. I was impatient to finish my training as a rookie so that I could have my own pair of horses to take care of. When I was finally drafted to my Company, at Bulford Camp in Wiltshire, I was issued with a pair of heavy draught horses of Flemish stock, chestnut in colour, who were named Harold and Maud. I adored them. During my two years' service I served as a Captain's groom, living in at his home away from camp, taking care of his charger, his wife's and his children's hack ponies and my own mount. I rode in the Royal Tournament at Olympia in the tandem team, riding my own mount with a lead horse.

Eventually I was demobbed and sent back to "civvy street" to seek a living. Seek a living—what an understatement! I walked the streets of London for months: according to the Establishment we were again in a financial crisis. Marvellous! I am sixty-two years young, and I cannot remember any year that the government of the day did not declare some sort of financial crisis. It amazes me: our universities turn out as many economists as Walls turn out sausages—but after all, what can you expect? It is the economics of capitalism they are taught, doomed to failure by reason of capitalism's lack of a central, planned economy, creating slump-boom-slump periods; it is the economics of the jungle.

After weeks and weeks of unemployment I finally managed to get a job as a hod-carrier to the bricklayers building a luxury cinema, the Brixton Astoria. It was pure bluff on my part—I had never seen a hod, let alone carried one. I dreaded Monday morning. But necessity is the mother of invention. I watched some of the hod-carriers packing their hods, and followed suit. But now I had to shoulder the thing and climb a forty-foot ladder and keep the bricklayers supplied with bricks (if the foreman bricklayer sees them waiting, you're for the high jump). But luck was with me. An experienced hod-carrier tumbled how green I was, and when I told him the whole story he became friendly and sympathetic, took me under his wing and became my tutor. I was given the job of looking after those bricklayers who were working at ground level until I had got the feel of the hod, and during my dinner-hour, under the tuition of my new-found friend, I practised climbing ladders with a loaded hod. I was an apt pupil and learned fast. But for many days I worked in fear, having been warned to keep my eyes open for scaffold-board traps—these are places where the boards don't overlap at the ends but only just meet; if you haven't kept your eyes open you step on the end, and that's your lot—down into space you fall. My friend told me that this was what had happened on the previous Friday to the man whose job I had taken . . . oh well! overcome your fear or become unemployed again, and I was saving to get married. By the time the cinema was nearing completion I had become an efficient labourer (and an eager trade unionist), and so the bricklayer foreman offered me a job on another site, and luck stayed with me for a while longer.

Winter came, which meant shorter working hours. Some of the bricklayers went off to look for inside jobs that were not affected by short daylight or frost. This meant, of course, a reduction in the number of hod-carriers. Once more I was out "on the stones", looking for work.

After a few weeks I obtained a job on the maintenance staff at Standard Telephones, Hendon, an American firm. My job was cleaning toilets, sweeping workshop floors and keeping the milling machines clear. Another class lesson: I had to spend more time and care on the clerical staff *toilets* than on the machine operators' *lavatories*—a quick sweep and a slosh down for those, pick up the newspaper—no toilet rolls for the workers! This all helped to create a barrier between the wage worker who punched a clock and the salaried employee who signed a book, and kept them divided. Then there were persons known as "chasers". Their job was to chase particular orders by finding out who the machine operators were. A Time and Motion Study team was introduced. Their job, we were told, was to see if they could reduce the movements made by the operator "to make it easier for him". How kind and human, I thought—until lunch time. Outside the factory gates, leaflets were being distributed, urging everyone to attend a meeting convened by some machine-operators who were members of the Communist Party factory "cell". (That's what they were called in those days; we have factory groups or branches now.) The purpose of the meeting was to explain what lay behind the Time and Motion Study— the danger of speed-up, leading to fewer jobs and more accidents at work. If my memory serves me rightly, it was called the Bedeaux system, after a French economist.

I went along and attended my first political meeting. And that was my first meeting with Communists.

In 1931, I married the girl-friend of my school-leaving days. We had a wonderful fortnight's honeymoon in Bournemouth, and returned to live in two rooms at Walworth—and we were fortunate in those days to get two rooms, even though they were in a basement, and to have got them so quickly as we did.

Back to work on Monday, sacked on Friday—a wonderful start to married life. But my young bride came from a good working-class family. She faced up to the problem and continued to work in order to make our marriage a happy and successful one; she went right on working up to the age of fifty and no doubt will be prepared to do so again should our economic problems become too difficult.

Show me a militant trade unionist and I'll gamble that behind him stands a militant wife. No sacrifice has been too demanding on my wife's loyalty as a mother, wife and comrade: and a militant political and industrial career can make very heavy demands on a man's free time and family life.

During this setback at the start of our marriage, Ellen went back to her former job while I went into the street, "on the knocker", peddling a household disinfectant, carbolic. In summer time there was a demand for it in those days, particularly in working-class areas.

However, the competition was too keen, and I couldn't get enough to put into the home to supplement Ellen's wages. Eventually I again found a job as a hod-carrier on a housing site where they were putting up private dwellings—jerry-built throughout from the footings to the gabled roof-tops. After two attempts to organise the labourers into the Union, I was sacked at the one o'clock start, cleaned up my hod, shovel and grafting-tool, tied them together, drew my cards and money, and went back home to wait for the wife. I had the kettle on ready for her arrival, gave her a lovely cup of steaming-hot tea, and then broke the news. Not a word of complaint. She just said: "You know what you're doing. You have to do the work."

During my spells of unemployment, I had found time to do some reading and political study. I joined the Labour Party, but I did not remain a member for long. One day, after signing on at the Walworth Road Labour Exchange, I found that the Unemployed Workers' Movement was holding a meeting. I stopped to listen. The speaker was a powerfully-built chap with a rugged countenance and a stentorian voice. He was explaining the reason for the mass unemployment and the need to get organised to demand an end to the Means Test and the closing down of the work camps—Belmont in particular. That was the place where you could be directed when you had exhausted your twenty-six weeks' miserable unemployment benefit; you made an application for relief and were then directed to this labour camp while your dependants were issued with food. The speaker went on to explain why there should be liaison between the Unemployed Workers' Movement and the trade unions. Each was dependent on the other, he said. If there was no political understanding, the unemployed would always be used as cheap labour as a constant threat to those in work, while we, the unemployed, needed the strength of the trade union movement to pressure the government into removing the Means Test and providing adequate maintenance and increased benefits.

All his made good sense to me, and when the speaker had finished his talk and answered questions from the crowd and the chairman had appealed for a collection and closed the meeting, I stayed behind. I'd been deeply impressed by all that had been said and wanted to continue the discussion with the speaker. Arising out of our conversation I learned that he was a casual dock-worker and his name was Patsy Hicks. We became friends, and as a result of many keen and heated discussions we had together, and the reading of some of the books he recommended to me, I began to do some political re-thinking.

Two of the books which deeply impressed me were Upton Sinclair's *The Jungle*, and Jack London's *The Iron Heel*. These two works of political fiction made me avid for political literature of all kinds, and I began to be a regular borrower at the Public Library. I should like to pay tribute here to a philanthropist called John Passmore Edwards who was, so I understand, the founder of the Public Libraries, or at any rate one of the founders. He was a benefactor to me all right. To my political-fiction reading I added *News from Nowhere* by William Morris, Robert Tressell's *The Ragged Trousered Philanthropists*, A. L. Cronin's *The Stars Look Down* and Steinbeck's *The Grapes of Wrath* and *In Dubious Battle*. On the non-fiction side I studied *The History of Mankind*, Thomas Paine's *Age of Reason* and *The Rights of Man* and

THE STRIKE FOR "THE DOCKERS' TANNER". SEAMEN AND COAL-
HEAVERS SHOW SUPPORT

DOCKERS AND THEIR WIVES IN THE 1889 STRIKE

WEDDING GROUP, 1931

Frederick Engels' *The Origin of the Family*. All this, with continuing discussion with different political thinkers, led me to join the National Unemployed Workers' Movement, whose chief founder and organiser was Wal Hannington. Hannington, in my opinion, was one of the great working-class fighters of the twentieth century. The present lot in the Labour Cabinet aren't fit to be compared with him for struggle, sacrifice and contribution to the struggle of the British labour movement. I can prove what I am saying. As I write these lines, my wife comes and shows me the headlines in the *Evening News*—*541,585 Jobless*, over the 2 per cent level of unemployment considered "healthy" by the unholy trinity Wilson, Brown and Gunter. Not a scrap of feeling for the untold misery and hardship that unemployment means to those 541,585 people and their families. Working-class leaders indeed! (Sorry for the digression—but I feel bitter and angry at the confidence trickstering that is used against our class.)

To continue about my newly-formed friendship with Patsy, I recall a very ugly incident that took place on a pay-day at the Walworth Road Labour Exchange. Anyone who has experienced prolonged unemployment knows that you leave home each morning with high hopes that if you search thoroughly, prepared to take any kind of work that is offered, something will turn up; but after continuous curt refusals, and sometimes even insults, you arrive back at the Labour Exchange tired, disappointed and on edge. Perhaps you may have got back a few minutes late. The clerk is officious and haughty, and maybe gives a sarcastic reply to the excuse you have offered. After the experiences of the morning you are feeling de-humanised and now comes a further insult—bang! you lose control and explode.

This is what happened to one poor chap on the day I am speaking of. He had just been informed by the clerk that he'd received his last unemployment benefit as he had exhausted the statutory twenty-six weeks, and must now make application for relief. The picture is still with me, the shock and frustration on his face, fear of the Means Test and perhaps being directed to Belmont Labour Camp—it was as if one were watching an Old Bailey trial and the judge had put on his black cap and announced the death sentence. For to be told that your little means of security for your wife and kids was now ended *was* like a death sentence. The poor chap stood there, his face drained of every vestige of colour, trembling with emotion, lost for words. Suddenly all his pent-up nervous energy was released in one great gush. He leapt over the counter, grabbed the unfortunate clerk by the collar and attempted to throttle him. All the other clerks came running to the aid of their colleague; on our side many fellow unfortunates rushed to assist one of their own. In a flash, the whole Exchange was in an uproar.

Meanwhile the Manager had telephoned Carter Street Police Station, which was nearby. Within a few minutes, in came the police, their truncheons at the ready. This is where Patsy's leadership came to the fore. He grabbed the Sergeant in charge and urged him not to use force, then turned and bellowed the same appeal to the rest of us. The Sergeant reacted favourably and ordered the truncheons to be put away. Then he and Patsy approached the unfortunate chap who had started it, and gradually soothed him. Patsy appealed to the manager and the clerk not to press charges, and after a discussion in the Manager's office both the two antagonists shook hands, order was restored, and the police left. This was one of my first experiences of the Unemployed Workers' Movement, and of the many capable stewards who led it.

3

Stepney, my Future Home

For once in a while, Dame Fortune smiled on my wife and me. I arrived home one day from the Labour Exchange in low spirits. I had started out with hopes of being issued with a green card to take along to a building site in the City. (You had to have a green card from the Exchange in order to be interviewed for a job.) But by the time my turn came, it was too late, the tickets had all gone.

When Ellen opened the street door she welcomed me with a radiant smile and a kiss, looking very excited. "I've got wonderful news," she said all in a rush. "Guess what's happened?"

I hazarded a guess or two but was way off the beam.

"We've been offered a house with five rooms!" Now she had me as excited as herself, for even in those days houses were hard to come by. Thousands of families were living in one or two rooms, with parents or strangers. "Where is it?" I asked.

Her face changed a little and excitement abated. "It's in East London, Stepney, next door to Auntie Rose."

It gave me a bit of a pang to think of leaving my own borough, where I had spent all my boyhood. But I couldn't resist my wife's smile—what husband can, particularly when he has only been married for a few months! And so we were soon busy, packing our bits and pieces in readiness for the moving-van and on the following Saturday we crossed to the northern bank of the Thames waterfront—a momentous step which has helped to shape the whole of my subsequent life and character.

The new chapter in our life-story starts, then, in a little five-roomed house with a garden and a railed front in St. Dunstan's Street (re-named Timothy Street a few years later) which runs parallel to the once-fashionable Burdett Road. In Stepney's rural times Burdett Road, lined with three-storied houses with big bay windows, flights of steps up to their front doors, and trees in the front gardens, had been occupied by the local gentry. By now the houses were mostly let out in tenements, with one here and there occupied by a doctor or veterinary surgeon. Near our street ran the Regent's Canal, along which timber-barges were towed by horses to various yards along the banks. My wife's Aunt Rose owned a little provision store a few doors from our house. So this was Stepney!—a borough to which I had come reluctantly, but one I have grown to love and in which I'll continue to live as long as I'm here.

What tremendous people lived, and still live, in Stepney's narrow streets; people full of character, native wit and Cockney shrewdness, with the community spirit still strong in them. In this day and age of skyscrapers and vast blocks of matchbox dwellings, visiting strangers can still feel at home amid its churches, Catholic and Protestant, its Methodist Mission, Chapels, Synagogues and Mosque; with two huge breweries, Charringtons and Mann & Crossmans supplying the countless pubs—and its sharp teenagers of both sexes who so impressed a well-known television personality that he remarked that the smartest-tailored youth in London, both for style and quality, were to be found in the East End.

Stepney, perhaps above all other London boroughs, has a long history of struggle. For it was at Mile End, in 1381, that Wat Tyler and his peasant rebels met King Richard II and forced him to agree to all their demands. A few days later Wat Tyler was stabbed at Smithfield by one of the King's followers, and the coat-of-arms of the City of London has a dagger in its right-hand corner to commemorate the murder of one of the bravest of our English peasantry, who dared to challenge the ruling establishment on behalf of human dignity and freedom.[1]

Shoot over to the Wapping side, consisting mostly of docks, wharves and warehouses, where nearly every other family is descended from Irish immigrant labourers who settled alongside

[1]Wat Tyler and his followers have been truthfully presented to the world by the famous composer Alan Bush, whose opera *Wat Tyler* had its premiere in the German Democratic Republic and has been performed there many times. So far the people of this country haven't had the opportunity to see it. Perhaps Miss Jennie Lee in her present job will recognise what the opera could do for our understanding of history. Or maybe the Farmers' Union might sponsor its presentation here?

the Thames in Wapping and St. George's. Families with sur-
names like Cassidy, O'Rourke, Kelly, McCarthy and Foley,
whose grandparents used to talk of having kissed the Blarney
Stone and seen the "Little People". Here in 1576 a Roman burial
ground was discovered; nearby, as a warning to sea pirates and
rovers, a gallows was erected, and the bodies of the executed
pirates were left swinging in the wind until three tides had swept
over them, after which they were removed to the eastern end
of the Wapping waterfront, still known as Execution Dock. It
served for two centuries. It was in Wapping, too, in the seven-
teenth century, that the notorious Hanging Judge Jeffreys went
to a Thames-side tavern for a bit of private revelry and,
although disguised, was recognised by a former prisoner he had
sentenced; he was seized by the Wapping citizens and imprisoned in the Tower, where he died during his incarceration.
Poetic justice!

From Wapping to Rotherhithe runs one of the finest feats of
nineteenth-century engineering, the first successful tunnel to be
built under the Thames, constructed by the Brunels, father and
son. An unknown number of the Irish settlers of St. George's
were killed or injured while working on it.

It was here in Stepney that the first big organised dock strike
took place—the 1889 strike, commonly referred to in our industry
as the strike for the "Dockers' Tanner", which not only increased
the pay and improved the conditions of the dockers but also
opened the portals of the T.U.C. to unskilled labour. At that
time the dockers, who were treated little better than beasts of
burden, had to fight and struggle daily for the casual work that
was handed out—for an hour or two's work given according to
the whim of the ship's foreman or harbour master on the quayside. There were hundreds of them, men with large families of
kids to feed, suffering from malnutrition and extreme poverty.
Those who were fortunate to obtain two hours' work would often
sell their second hour to another man because they were too weak
to complete the job; with their hour's pay and the proceeds of
this transaction they would make for the nearest eating-house,
put some food inside themselves and take the rest home to their
families. Conditions were so terrible that the religious bodies and
Christian organisations were stirred into action; in the borough
of Stepney and adjacent waterside areas soup kitchens were set
up in the streets to feed the striking dockers. The conscience of

the whole nation was aroused. Victory was won, and the 6d. an hour was granted.

Up to the time of the 1889 strike, membership of the T.U.C. had been confined exclusively to the skilled guilds and craft unions. Now the unskilled were represented on that body—in my opinion a very important result of the struggle.

Again in Stepney, a dock strike took place that changed a government's policy in international affairs. This was after 1917, when the working people of Russia took the decision to end the despotic rule of the Czar and the corruption of the landowners and employers, set up their own government for "Peace, Bread and Land" and published the secret treaties. Great mass meetings and demonstrations left no doubt as to the sympathy of the British workers; but the government was openly hostile to the new Soviet Republic. In 1919 there was widespread opposition to the action of the Lloyd George Government in sending an expedition to Archangel against the Bolsheviks; soldiers mutinied and refused to go to this new front. The formation of a national "Hands off Russia" Committee forced the government to withdraw its forces and stop direct intervention. But it continued to send money and supplies to the White armies who were fighting against the Soviet Government. This indirect intervention reached its highest point when Poland was encouraged to invade Russia in 1920. The British workers replied by setting up Councils of Action, and then came the *Jolly George* incident that made the London dockers famous throughout the world. The *Jolly George* was being loaded with munitions that were to be shipped to Poland; when the dockers discovered the nature of the packing-cases that were lying on the quayside waiting to be loaded, they sent a deputation to Fred Thompson and Ernest Bevin—the London and General Secretaries of the Dockers' Union—and received assurances that the Union would stand by them if they took strike action. This has been described by Harry Pollitt, the late General Secretary of the Communist Party, who at that time was working in the dock and was a member of the Boilermakers' Union. Fred Thompson's account is more detailed. The London District of the Dockers' Union decided to prevent the transport of munitions to Poland by all means in their power. This decision was sent to the Executive, but as it failed to find endorsement, the London dockers decided to act on their own. Every dock and wharf was combed for munitions, and action was centred on the

Jolly George. The dockers were determined to stop this ship at all costs. They decided to render the ship unseaworthy before taking action. This was done by putting such a list on her that it would be unsafe to move her, even in the dock. Then at the agreed time, every docker in the ship and on the quayside ceased work.

What developed next was like a fast game of football. The London lads had kicked off for their side; the ball passed to the dockers in other European ports, who began by taking similar action. In Ireland, the Dublin dockers refused to *unload* munitions intended for use against their own Nationalists. The Irish railwaymen entered the game by refusing to move any train containing British troops or ammunition. Back to Britain. The (old, militant) *Daily Herald* printed the name of every ship bound for Poland. The T.U.C., in spite of the opposition of Jimmy Thomas, decided that unless the government withdrew its troops from Ireland and ceased its support for Poland they would call a general strike. And all over Europe, dockers and railwaymen, inspired by the *Jolly George* incident, refused to handle arms for Poland. The British government caved in and there was no war.

It was the poverty in East London, Stepney in particular, that moved a young medical student, Thomas John Barnardo, to try and help the many thousands of young homeless children who had been left to fend for themselves. Shocked by the poverty and squalor, the slums full of starving children whose sole means of existence was to sell matches, shine shoes, beg, steal or turn over dustbins for scraps; horrified at the indifference of London's society to this misery and suffering, his pity and anger moved him into a mission that was to become his life's work. He became an outstanding pioneer in child welfare.

In 1866, in a disused donkey-stable in Hope Street, he set up an evening school for ragged children where, in shelter and warmth, he taught them the simple basics of reading and writing. It became the talk of Stepney, and in no time his stable-school was flooded with homeless waifs and strays. His friend Samuel Smith, a member of Parliament, lent him £1,000, and in a few short months, in Stepney Causeway, he set up his first Home for twenty-five homeless boys. Its reputation spread all over the East End and countless requests for accommodation were received. He was at first afraid to expand, lest he should run into debt. But then a tragedy happened. Dr Barnardo had to refuse accommodation to a child, though he gave him money to tide him over until there was a vacancy. But before room could be found for him the boy, nicknamed "Carrots", died of exposure. From that time onward, a sign was placed over the Stepney Causeway home which read "No Destitute Child Ever Refused Admission".

One of his greatest contributions to the care of children was his determination to de-institutionalise his "homes" by building several cottages instead of one vast building. Here the kids could live in "families", from toddlers to teenagers, each helping in the welfare of the others; a "mother" was put in charge of each cottage. At the time of his death in 1905 Dr Barnardo's family numbered over 7,000 and 60,000 children had passed through his ever-open doors.

Is it to be wondered at, that on moving into this historical borough, so rich in humanism, I should be affected by its background. I was becoming a keen student of politics and an active trade unionist. And at once I began to come into contact with workers whose names were household words—men like the late Pat Coleman, organiser of Stepney's anti-fascist groups: Ted Dickens, one of the best-known unofficial dock leaders, who stood trial at the Old Bailey for his trade union principles; Wally Jones, another grand dock fighter. There was Phil Piratin, Stepney's first Communist councillor, later to become a Member of Parliament and join with Willie Gallacher, whose advice and counsel in dock struggles were so often sought in the House of Commons lobbies, and never refused. Tubby Rosen, Arnold Posner, Barney Borman, Max Levitas—all these lads have organised thousands of Stepney people into tenants' organisations, led by that tireless and lovable character, known in every part of Tower Hamlets, Solly Kaye. Their names, and the organised might of the tenants' associations, would strike fear into Stepney landlords to the tune of thousands of pounds in repairs and reduced rents. Last but not least was Nat Cohen, a Stepney trade unionist and one of the first British volunteers to join the International Brigade fighting the fascists in Spain.

If I have left other names out it is because they are too numerous to mention. Stepney in that period abounded with working-class fighters. Every night at familiar street corners you could stand and listen to them speaking at meetings, Labour men and Communists and leaders of the Unemployed Workers' Movement—that was the way to learn politics! On street corners, at dock and factory gates—not sitting round the television set listening to

the cultured voices of the Establishment having the bloody nerve
to tell the workers what's wrong with their industries!

It would do the leadership of the Labour Party good to
remember that its growth and development into the largest single
working-class party in Britain began with street-corner meetings.
If the Left-wing Labour M.P.s were to get outside the factory
and dock gates, the pit-heads and the shipyards and call on the
organised industrial workers to support their challenge to the
Right-wing appeasers led by the unholy Trinity of Wilson, Brown
and Gunter* and stand up to L.B.J. and Washington and the
financial Gnomes of Zurich—if this were done, the winds of
change would take on the velocity of a hurricane and make room
for a leadership deeply rooted in the British working class, conscious of the road it must take to build a socialist Britain by
putting an end to class-collaboration.

The men and women who *produce*, the wage earners and the
salaried workers, the civil servants, teachers, scientists, the
dockers and merchant seamen, ship-builders and repairers, fisher-
men, railwaymen, workers in road transport, aviation, medical
and hospital establishments—these are the people who are responsible for the wealth and prosperity of the nation. We are
many, they are few.

---

* When I started writing my memoirs, these three were the unholy trinity.
Today, it is Wilson, Jenkins and Castle and I might rather call them the Three
Witches, with Castle as the Sorcerer's Apprentice stirring the witches' brew.
By the time the book is published, it may be others—who knows?

4

Stepping out to Maturity

In one of my unemployed spells I was conned by some of my pals, who knew I had done a bit of boxing in the army, to have a go at earning some money by fighting professionally. I listened to their con, and went to see the promoter of the famous Blackfriars Ring. I walked into his office and told him I wanted to fight. He asked me if I had fought professionally before, and if I had a manager. I truthfully told him no. He suggested that I should turn up at the evening show, sit in the substitutes' box and wait to be called if one of the billed contestants failed to appear; providing I was the right weight or thereabouts I would be called as a substitute. Payment for this was, for six rounds, 25s. a win; £1 lose or draw, and if you made a good showing you might be billed on the next occasion. Out of this fee you paid 2s. each to your seconds, 1s. to the dressing-room attendant, and the rest was yours. I was skint, newly married, and anxious to do justice to my young wife who was the only breadwinner. So I turned up that evening and took my place in the substitutes' box, as nervous as a kitten and hoping I would not be called. But fate was kind to me—or unkind, according to your point of view.

One of the officials came to the box and beckoned me. This was it! I went to the dressing room and jumped onto the scales. In walked the doctor and I had the speediest "medical" of my life "Get ready, son, you're on next!" I stripped, put on some trunks and a pair of slippers. Boxing boots?—you're kidding! Only top and second raters could afford those. I sat waiting, with the proverbial butterflies dancing away a million to the second, not daring to think. A voice shouted: "You're on, son!" and away I went, scared to death but determined to make a show in order to be billed.

I climbed up into the corner and sat on the stool provided

while the seconds laced the gloves, my old raincoat over my shoulders. Dressing gown?—that again was for those at the top of the bill, the fifteen-rounders with managers. There I sat, nervous and scared, not of the physical hurt, but as to what sort of a show I was going to put up—for apart from a few fights in the army I had never been even in an amateur club. My opponent was a fully-fledged professional with much experience. In those days of mass unemployment those chaps would take any distance, six, ten or fifteen rounds, come what may, so long as there was a living to be got at it. They would fight three or four times a week; this was possible because there was professional boxing in every London borough every night. Competition was tremendous, and the substitutes' box was never without seasoned campaigners waiting for a chance to earn a few bob. Raw youngsters like me were referred to as Hungry Fighters—and rightly so; to most of us it wasn't a career, it was a living and we were fighting for a crust.

The bell went. There I was, out in the middle, and as far as experience went I didn't know what day it was. But a few sharp jolts to my head and body livened me up, and although I lost it must have been a reasonably good show, for when it ended money was thrown into the ring by the crowd. "Nobbings" was the term for it, appreciation by the spectators for a good game fight. The cash was picked up by your seconds while you were on your way to the dressing-room and handed to you afterwards, and of course you did not question their honesty. I recall an occasion when one of the contestants blew his top, saying that he had seen several half-crowns being thrown in. "Don't be silly," he was told. "With all that blood in your eyes, you couldn't tell half-crowns from pennies."

My sojourn in the fight game didn't last long—about a dozen bouts, and I lost more than I won. My wife used to wait up at nights to bathe my eyes and ears. I came to the conclusion that the fight game was not for me.

After a further spell of unemployment I got a job hod-carrying on a building site in the City, for the largest building contractors in Britain, J. Mowlem Limited. It was to be my first step towards trade union maturity—the step when the individual develops from being a mere card-holder into an active trade union member. That is to say, he recognises the shortcomings of the site—the lack of 100 per cent trade union membership, working operations, safeguards and general amenities not in conformity with the rules laid down to the trade union or the Factory Acts—and sets about to correct them. The first important step is to challenge the other workers to show their trade union cards and, with the help of those who are members, to bring the job up to 100 per cent; then to hold meetings for the election of a site committee, and next approach the general foreman and discuss the irregularities with a view to getting them put right.

On the Monday morning when I started, I had just finished reading that famous classic of trade union literature, *The Ragged Trousered Philanthropists* by Robert Tressell, and was all stirred up and ready to have a go. I first approached a fellow-hod-carrier, showed him my card and asked him to do the same. Happily for me, he produced his, which gave me confidence to approach others. Those were the days when Irish immigrant labour was spreading. Raw Catholic lads from Connemara and Galway were driven through poverty to come over to this country to seek a living and send money home to their families. The building workers referred to them as "two-for-half-a-crown"—it had been rumoured that they would approach the general foreman on a job and offer to work for half a crown an hour between two of them—half a crown being the hourly rate for the average single labourer. How true this was I do not know, but like all racial minorites they were *scapegoats*—today it is our coloured brothers, who are dehumanised and insulted with such labels as coons and wogs, potential trade unionists who with half a chance can become as militant and solid as the Irish lads who today play a leading part second to none on the building sites.

My card inspection revealed that out of the twelve hod-carriers only three were not union members, and they promised to join. I next approached the navvies—the general labourers responsible for getting the footings out and the excavation, cutting trenches for the bricklayers to start laying out. Not one of them had a card, but after a few hours of consistent discussion in the dinner-breaks I won them over to joining. By the end of the week, and with the co-operation of the bricklayers' card-steward, the site had become 100 per cent trade union. It was from this effort that I qualified for the Tolpuddle Medal, which was sent me with a citation signed by Walter Citrine and Herbert Morrison. I wrote back telling of my pride and gratitude at receiving such an honour, but drawing attention to the fact that I was a member of the Communist Party, the organisation which they frequently denounced as a "disrupter" of the trade union movement. I suggested that in view of my award they should publicly retract this accusation against the Party. I never received any answer.

Yes, I had become a member of the Communist Party, a step of tremendous importance in the shaping of my life towards political maturity. I remember the day I signed up. I had been taking part in one of the actions organised by the National Unemployed Workers' Movement. After this event was over I went home and did the housework. My wife was working right across London, in Acton. It was a long journey for her; she used to leave home at 6.30 in the morning and arrive back about 7 in the evening and if I was not working myself I made a point of being at home to welcome her with a pot of freshly-made tea. It is the countless women like my wife, in the ranks of the working class, who provide the reason why divorce is much less frequent among us than in the upper strata. The reason is that our wives are evaluated differently. A good working-class wife is not only a lover; she can cook, sew, darn, mend, take care of the kids—no nannies or boarding schools—manage well on meagre wages or the dole, and is prepared to go to work part- or full-time to help out. Marriage is a partnership based not on dowries, banking accounts and social position but on shared responsibility, companionship and sacrifice.

So there I was with a nice pot of tea waiting for Ellen, and after the evening meal I helped her with the washing up and told her I was off to a meeting. She didn't complain. I made my way to Eric Street, where the Stepney Communist Party held regular Wednesday meetings. In those days you were fortunate to be able to learn your politics not from some cultured voice and face on a television screen but at the street corners from working-class lads and lasses in industry, and what they said you could relate to actual living experience.

I arrived in time to hear the chairman introduce the main speaker, Pat Devine. He was to speak about the war in Spain, where the people were defending their democratically-elected government against the insurgents led by General Franco (who had the support of arms, equipment and troops provided by Hitler and Mussolini). Nazi and Italian fascist air pilots were obtaining military flying experience bombing Spanish cities and towns and battling with the ill-equipped and poorly-armed Republican forces, the People's Army. In keeping with international law, the Chamberlain government had the duty to provide the legal government of Spain with the arms it required to put down the insurrection. But it had taken shelter behind the farcical pretext of "Non-Intervention" and the Spanish people were left to fight, with incredible bravery, not merely against a handful of treacherous generals and their Moorish troops but against the full force of German and Italian fascism. The call had gone out to the British labour movement to bring pressure to bear on the government and stop this wicked policy. Meanwhile the ordinary working folk, all their class instinct aroused to the dangers of fascism, had rushed to aid the Spanish people. Ambulances, food, medical supplies, every kind of aid (short of the forbidden arms that were so desperately needed) were being sent in an ever-growing flood, built up from the pennies and sixpences of people who had a job themselves to make ends meet. And men had gone too, risking and giving their lives in that great upsurge of solidarity that built the International Brigades.

This was the subject of Pat Devine's speech. Gazing at this well-built, fine-looking man with his outdoor complexion, for the next thirty minutes I was held spellbound by his Irish brogue his magnificent oratory, but above all by what he was saying.

After he had finished, the chairman introduced Nat Cohen, who had just returned from the Spanish front badly wounded. Still not fully recovered, he was assisted to the platform and in a quiet but passionate voice told us about the terrible events taking place in Spain.

The chairman brought the meeting to a close with the customary appeal for people to join the Communist Party. A small, dark-haired woman held out a form to me, and I could resist no longer. Pat Devine and Nat Cohen between them had convinced me. I signed, and handed the form back to Beattie Marks—a grand comrade who still, thirty years after that night, continues to do consistent Party work and (though well over retiring age) to give her services in the office at King Street. An example to the youth.

I went home, sat down to my supper, and told my wife I had joined the Party. She replied with that typical phrase, said countless times by loyal working-class wives: "Well, you know what you're doing!"

It was in that same summer of 1937 that Sir Oswald Mosley, leader of the British Union of Fascists, announced his decision to march through the East End of London with his Blackshirt followers. But the East End decided otherwise. Herbert Morrison and other Labour Party leaders advised their followers to stay at home, but the Communist Party, the London Trades Council, the local trades councils, trade unionists and co-operators organised Town's Meetings, street-corner meetings, and the slogan "They Shall Not Pass" was chalked and white-washed on every available wall in Stepney.

On the eve of the proposed march, the streets leading to Gardiners' Corner and Aldgate East were filled with tremendous activity. Throughout the night the Stepney folk, Jew and Gentile from all walks of life—dockers, stevedores, tailors, engineers, ship repairers, council workers, busmen, railwaymen, trade unionists, members of the Labour Party, the Co-operative Party and the Communist Party with their wives and kids were busy lugging and hauling old furniture, bed springs, tables and chests of drawers out into the streets, building barricades. They used anything they could lay hands on, packing cases, old fish boxes which found their way from nearby Billingsgate fish market, stopping only for a pot of tea or a bottle of light ale bought on the point of closing-time. Songs were sung, plenty of working-class banter was exchanged among the barricade builders and finally, when Sunday dawned, Stepney was ready to prevent the fascist march into the East End, cradle of London's industrial and socialist movements.

"*No Pasaran!* They Shall Not Pass!" From early morning the people of London began to gather, until by two o'clock the streets and roads leading in from the City to the East End were packed with a solid mass of people, arms linked, all with one slogan on their lips. "They Shall Not Pass."

It looked as if the entire police force of Greater London had been mobilised to protect Mosley and his battalion, and there were hundreds of mounted police with their long truncheons, preparing to smash the barricade of human flesh. As the time drew near for the arrival of the fascists, you could feel the tightening of muscle and sinew and the bracing of thighs and calves hardened and toughened in industry. Suddenly there was a hushed silence, as the strains of the fascist marching song were heard and, coming from the direction of the City, the crowds saw the black-shirted, jack-booted legion, carrying swastika banners and, in the centre, the Union Jack borne by specially-selected, tall, blond youths on either side of their Fuhrer and his henchmen, strutting with military arrogance.

The roar that went up from the East End barricades, bastions of London's labour movement, was like a peal of thunder. Hell and fury broke loose as the Metropolitan and City police, under orders, began to rush the crowd to let Mosley and his fascists march through. But everyone stood firm. Each time a gap was made by the police with their swinging truncheons, it was speedily re-formed. Running fights took place, with skirmishes in the back streets. Mounted police made repeated charges, marbles were thrown into the road and the horses slipped and slid like beginners at a skating rink. The road was littered with dislodged helmets. But heads were everywhere. There were tremendous fights round the Black Marias where men, women and youths were being scruffed and frog-marched face down and literally slung in. (*Your police are so wonderful!*)

But they did not pass. With cuts and blood and broken limbs the slogan was fulfilled. And who among us ever imagined that within three short years those very people who had to appear in local police courts to be fined or imprisoned for "disturbing the peace" or "preventing the police from carrying out their duties" would again be showing the same courage and determination, the same passion for freedom and democracy as they faced up to the bombardment of their homes, the factories and docks of London's East End. Where one house in every three was to suffer bomb damage, where women and kids, with their cheery Cockney defiance, kicked the incendiary bombs out of the way when no stirrup pumps were available.

It was a magnificent victory. But 1937 was a tragic year for the British working class. In two of the fiercest battles of the Spanish war, Jarama and Brunete, some of the flower of the trade union movement, Communists and members of the Labour Party, gave their lives. Today, thirty years later, let me pay tribute to these gallant comrades and brothers who died defending democracy in Spain, with an extract from a memorial souvenir published in 1938 in honour of the British Battalion of the 15th Brigade:

"Out of the proud traditions of Britain's past they came, part of the long struggle for freedom carried forward from Wat Tyler, through men like Byron and movements like the Chartists, through Keir Hardie to the present day. Our modern bearers of Great Britain's traditions came forward to answer the call, ready to give their lives that freedom might live."

I say to all members of the labour movement today: do not despair of the present situation in our trade union and Labour leadership. I am confident that there exists within our present rank-and-file men and women, brothers and sisters, who will rise to the occasion as these forerunners did in 1936–39, who will defeat the Wilsons, Gunters, Browns and knights of the T.U.C. round table, architects of the Prices and Incomes Policy with its legislation of fines and imprisonment, and rise up to build a socialist Britain. To the gallant men of the British Battalion— Salud!

During 1938 I was in and out of employment, unable to hold down any job for long because of my trade union convictions and activities. It was while I was working on the Odeon Cinema in Bow Road that I led my first strike. One of the trade union rulings stated that hod-carriers who had to climb any ladder over forty feet long must receive height or danger money to be paid at the rate of 2d. per hour. Our approach to the general foreman for this payment was turned down flat. I went home that evening dead needled. My wife, Ellen, noticed my mood, as wives do—they assess your moods in a flash and are nearly always right. She asked me about it, and when I told her, she said: "Why don't you call in the Union? That's what it's for!"

I rose next morning determined to make the challenge. I got to the site a little earlier than usual and, called all the hod-carriers together for a fresh discussion. It was agreed that we should make another approach to the general foreman. We did so, but when we told him of our intention to call in an official of the Union he was arrogant, and would not budge from his position of the previous day. So, at break time I called all the lads together. After further discussion a vote was put for strike action, resulting in a majority decision for a stoppage. I went and informed the general foreman of our decision. At midday, we held talks with the general labourers who promised to support us by refusing to unload the lorries which brought the bricks, cement, timber and other materials to the site. The bricklayers too pledged their support and by 1 p.m. the site was at a standstill.

The general foreman had by now modified his arrogant attitude. He sent for our committee, and after keen talks it was agreed that the height and danger moneys should be paid. We went along to tell the lads of this decision. But now it was our turn to be a bit cocky. They decided that we would only start if the payment were retrospective from the time when we first claimed it; and there was to be no loss of wages for the hours not worked because of his refusal.

Back we went. The foreman was seething with rage and humiliation, but he was up against a time factor. The site was behind schedule. Like a truculent schoolboy, he agreed, and work was resumed.

We were all elated at our success, and I went home very excited at my first experience of playing a leading part in the working-class struggle for the dignity of labour and recognition of our value to society. My elation was to be short lived, however, for the very next day I had to undergo another first experience. That was victimisation—but done in such a way that I could not prove it. It happened this way. Ever since the start of the job, the time-clerk had been fairly sympathetic and had winked an eye at five or ten minutes' lateness here or there. The general foreman never arrived on the site until about 8.30 a.m. But on the morning after his humiliation he turned up bang on time, eight o'clock sharp. I didn't. I arrived five minutes late, and was sacked at an hour's notice for bad time-keeping.

A very much happier event took place in that same year of 1938, however. Ellen gave birth to our first child, a lovely baby girl. We named her Kathleen and she has since grown into a very lovely person, both in looks and character. She is now married to the son of a docker, and they have two beautiful children.

I felt very proud of Kathleen when she telephoned me not long ago to tell me that she would be taking part in her first Communist Party demonstration, a "Peace in Vietnam" poster parade right in the heart of middle-class territory at Old Bexley, Kent—and taking her children along too.

5

The Eve of War

Towards the end of 1938 and the beginning of 1939, the activity
of the National Unemployed Workers' Movement took some
really spectacular forms, with the campaign for extra winter
relief for all unemployed workers and their families. In the
previous year the Government had been compelled by the
organised pressure of the workers—employed and unemployed
alike—to recognise that the "dole" was sharply decreasing in
value. (*Reynolds News* on July 18, 1937, estimated that in the
previous twelve months the purchasing power of the £1 had
fallen to 16s. 5d.) Instructions were issued to local Assistance
Board officials to "deal with any cases of hardship which may
arise in these circumstances".

It was left to the discretion of the local officials as to *how* they
should deal with these hardship cases. A few miserable shillings
were doled out to some claimants (in many cases, as little as 1s. a
week) and each claimant was told that the increase was made
because of changes in the prices of certain commodities". But
in April 1938 the Government stopped this extra grant on the
grounds that it had been made as a 'winter relief grant".

A fresh campaign, inside and outside Parliament, forced the
Government to make amends for this piece of trickery, and in
November 1938 it brought out a so-called "Winter Adjustment
Regulation" empowering local U.A.B. officials—again at their
discretion—to meet the claims of those who could prove "special
need" up to a maximum of 3s. a week extra. Needless to say,
hundreds of thousands of unemployed workers were informed
that they had no special needs in the winter months, with prices
still rising!

The N.U.W.M. started a new national campaign demanding
extra winter relief for *all* unemployed. Local agitation compelled

officials to grant relief to many to whom it had previously been refused. But as Christmas approached, it was felt that dramatic action needed to be taken to arouse the public conscience.

Today's sit-downs, organised by the ban-the-bomb C.N.D. and the Committee of One Hundred, led by that vigorous peace fighter Bertrand Russell, bring back sharp recollections of that winter campaign. Ours was not a sit-down but a lie-down—in Piccadilly Circus, flat on our backs in the snow, with posters on our chests which read: "Winter Relief for the Unemployed!" "End the Means Test!" "Work or Full Maintenance!" The traffic chaos stretched for miles, and as fast as the police picked us up, others took our places.

I recall the demonstration outside Stepney Labour Exchange, in Settle Street, where some of our members chained themselves to the railings, shouting slogans against the Means Test. Those of us who had done the padlocking stood by with the keys in our pockets and watched the police file the chains off.

As a follow-up to this action, we decided to invade the Ritz Hotel in Piccadilly. Everything was well planned. The press—that is, the London and national newspapers (and in those days before the swallowing up of the little fish by the big 'uns under free enterprise there was quite a number of them) were all informed in advance. At the appointed time about 150 of our unemployed members, all dressed up in such remnants of our best suits as had escaped the pawnbroker, walked quietly into the Grill and sat down. This did not have quite the hoped-for effect, for due to a mistake—the only organisational mistake I can remember on the part of the campaign committee—we had overlooked the fact that the Grill was never open in the afternoons, only in the evenings. However, we continued as planned, took our places at the tables which were being set by waiters in readiness for the evening, and then pulled out our posters from beneath our coats, with slogans calling for an end to the Means Test and more winter relief for the aged pensioners.

Can you imagine the looks on the faces of the waiters! They stood still in their tracks. Up rushed the management supervisor demanding to know what it was all about. He was politely told by our elected speaker, Wal Hannington, that we would like to be served with some tea and sandwiches because we were very tired and hungry, but he was not to be anxious and could present the bill which would be paid on the spot.

When the supervisor regained his breath he said, in a very cultured, precise Oxford-English voice: "I cannot permit you to be served. You are not our usual type of customer. You know full well that you are not accustomed to dine in an establishment of this quality. If you do not leave I shall have to send for the police." (This had already been done.) In reply, our spokesman informed him that many was the Saturday when wealthy clients of the Ritz would drive down to the East End workmen's caffs in their Rollses and Daimlers and have a jolly hot saveloy, old boy, what! Slumming, they called it, and they too were in unusual attire and frequenting establishments that were not accustomed to such a clientele; nevertheless, said our spokesman, these gentlemen were treated with courtesy and civility and nobody sent for the police. The Ritz, he added, was not a private members' club but a public restaurant; he requested the supervisor to give orders to the staff to serve us with the refreshment we had asked for.

The appeal might just as well have been addressed to the chandelier which hung from the ceiling. The supervisor stood there with a look of scorn, waiting for the police to come and throw us out. We refused to budge, insisting on our right as members of the general public, with legal tender in our pockets, to be served with what we had ordered. Meanwhile Wally had mounted the orchestra-platform to address us; waiters and kitchen staff stood around dumbfounded at our temerity. But our speaker was incensed and in good form, and the issue of class privilege was clearly put. I noticed several of the staff members nodding their heads as the speaker touched on salient points. His speech was never finished, however, for the Grill was soon surrounded by police. A couple of Inspectors came over and consulted our organisers; we were ordered to leave, and did so in an orderly manner. As we filed out several of the waiters came up to wish us luck in our campaign, and pressed money into our hands.

It was the week before Christmas. The Movement decided to send a petition to the King, asking him to use his royal prerogative to intervene with his Ministers on behalf of the unemployed. The petition was presented at Buckingham Palace—not without great difficulty.

Here is its text, which I quote from Wal Hannington's book *The Lean Years*.

"To His Majesty King George VI our humble petition:—We, your subjects, representatives of the National Unemployed Workers' Movement, humbly appeal to you on behalf of the unemployed in London and Great Britain to use your Royal Prerogative with your Government Ministers to grant Christmas relief to the unemployed and their families. Already in the Commons your Government Ministers have refused to give consideration to this plea, and each refusal will mean that millions of your subjects will suffer cold and hunger during the festive season. Our organisation has already been compelled to draw public attention to the needs of the unemployed by the lie-down strike action at Oxford Circus and the Ritz Hotel. We now appeal to Your Majesty in these last hours before Christmas Day to intervene with your Ministers in such a way that every unemployed family has fire in the grate and a Christmas dinner."

We awaited developments from our petition, which followed some days later (after the Christmas holidays had expired). All that happened was a reply from the Palace which said:

"The Private Secretary is commanded by the King to acknowledge the letter of December addressed to him, which by the King's instructions has been referred to His Majesty's responsible advisers."

Christmas Day was not allowed to pass without appropriate action. Outside the London residence of Lord Rushcliffe, Chairman of the Unemployed Assistance Board, 150 unemployed "carol-singers" assembled with posters and songs to remind him of this festive day that the unemployed were still hungry. After an hour they were removed by the police.

Just before the New Year, it was decided to use the famous Fire of London Monument for publicity. One morning, as the thousands of City workers commuting from Kent and Surrey streamed over London Bridge, they saw, hanging from the top of the Monument, a long, wide streamer with read: "For a Happy New Year, the Unemployed Must not Starve in 1939". This was eventually removed by the City police, who had to climb the three-hundred-and-odd stairs to do so. Great publicity was obtained, and the London newspapers were full of photographs.

This action was immediately followed by another and even more spectacular one. Again I quote from *The Lean Years*:

"The activity which crashed into the news on a still bigger

scale than anything we had done before took place on the night of December 31st, the day following the Monument episode. We knew that on this day the traditional crowds would assemble around midnight in the West End of London to celebrate the coming of the New Year; there would be general merriment in the hotels and on the streets. We decided to break through this facade of prosperity and happiness in such a way as not to seriously offend the general public and yet at the same time drive home to the public conscience the problem of unemployment. We fixed on the idea of a funeral procession through the West End at midnight with a black coffin. The call went out to our London branches to send groups of members to take part in this funeral procession and to mobilise for it in Trafalgar Square. From all over London they came, hundreds of them, although the call was not made until the day of the activity. The organisation was perfect. The police had no knowledge of it, special banners had been hurriedly made, and various paraphernalia from all sources had been dug out, including glass-sided hearse lanterns with lighted candles to give a deeper sense of reality to the "funeral". The coffin itself was conveyed to Trafalgar Square without being exposed to the public gaze until the appropriate moment arrived. An hour before midnight the "mourners" who had been gathering in the vicinity of the Square suddenly began to fall into procession ranks. The coffin was revealed, and on its sides was painted in large white letters the words "HE DID NOT GET WINTER RELIEF". The pall-bearers shouldered the coffin, the lamps were lit, heads were uncovered and the "funeral march" commenced. Thousands on the pavements gaped with amazement. The whole thing was being done so realistically that many of the onlookers were deceived into believing it was a real funeral procession, and they uncovered their heads. As the procession moved towards the Strand, they read the words on the coffin and saw the strange symbols and slogans which were being carried, and realised that it was a protest of the unemployed. Huge crowds followed in the wake of the "cortège". The sombre black coffin made a striking contrast to the gay colours of the revellers and the glittering lights of the West End. The procession was heading for St Paul's. But when it reached the Aldwych the police became alarmed and finally forbade it to proceed along Fleet Street. Perhaps they were afraid there would be an attempt to carry the coffin into the Cathedral. The coffin idea struck home.

The press reported it sensationally, and people became more aware of the conditions of the unemployed. Three days' later the coffin was delivered to 10 Downing Street."

On another occasion a plan was worked out for selected members to lie down on the rails in front of the "Golden Arrow" at Victoria Station. This could not be carried out, however, for the police were heavily guarding all the entrances to the station— it was the day Neville Chamberlain was to leave for his meeting with the Fascist dictator Mussolini. However, our members put up a valiant fight outside the station, shouting "Appease the unemployed, not Mussolini!".

The campaigns of the N.U.W.M. continued with never a let-up right to the outbreak of the second world war and for a time afterwards.

The appeasement policy of the Chamberlain government took us swiftly down the last stages of that slippery slope. Without one shot being fired Austria, Czechoslovakia, the Sudetenland were handed over to Hitler. The Communist Party was out in the forefront of the fight to prevent fascism from launching its terrible destruction, organising mass public meetings and demonstrations, denouncing the appeasement policy of the Tories. The voice of our Willie Gallacher, the one Communist fighter in Parliament, was raised in sole protest against the Munich sell-out and Chamberlain's "peace in our time".

Night after night you swallowed your tea and went out "on the knocker" warning, agitating, selling pamphlets written by (the late) Professor J. B. S. Haldane, urging the need for deep underground shelters to protect the people.

6

With the Fire Brigade

When war was declared, I went along to the recruiting office in Whitehall to volunteer for the Navy, but I was informed that I would have to wait for my age group. So meanwhile (I thought it was meanwhile but it turned out to be "for the duration") I went and volunteered for the Auxiliary Fire Service (A.F.S.) and was stationed in an L.C.C. school in Bow Road, Stepney.

Duties were forty-eight hours on, twenty-four hours off. It was organised, like the parent body, the London Fire Brigade, along Royal Navy lines. The station personnel were divided into three watches, red, white and blue. I was on the red watch. Discipline was like that in the forces: if you committed a misdemeanour you were put on a charge and appeared before the Divisional Superintendent, a high-ranking officer. Under escort, you would listen while the charge was read out, speak in defence, be marched out, brought back in, and then told your punishment—which could be from one to seven days' suspension without pay and drafting to another station. Nevertheless, the London Fire Brigade was served by a very progressive trade union under the leadership of John Horner, an able and progressive man of left-wing persuasion and a fine, down-to-earth orator, who was fortunate to have Executive members of the same progressive thinking as himself. All this was enriched by the entry of the newcomers who joined the A.F.S. and became members of the Fire Brigade Union, coming in with trade union experience gained in industry—engineers, electricians, building workers, dockers, teachers, etc.

I was eventually elected trade union delegate for my station and was responsible for collecting contributions and representing the personnel in negotiations with the station officer.

During the period of the London blitz, the men and women of

D

the A.F.S. performed deeds of heroism and sacrifice. At the time when the blitz was at its heaviest, with continual raids night after night, when our city was alight with the second Fire of London, the toll of dead and wounded was higher than that of any single British regiment in that period.

Volunteers were scarce. The government declared that the Fire Service was to become a fourth arm of defence, and ordered a conscripted service and a complete reorganisation of the A.F.S. which ended up with the absorption of all the professional fire brigades serving the major towns and cities into one National Fire Service. This played a tremendous role throughout the war years, not only as a fire-fighting service but during the political struggle for the opening of the Second Front. The Union executive, with the support of the rank and file, repeatedly raised its voice to this end, lobbying the House of Commons, moving resolutions at T.U. conferences. On many occasions during the black-out I recall going out with the lads from the station, white-washing slogans on pavements and walls—"Open the Second Front Now!"

To help the war production effort, the Fire Brigades Union was successful in negotiating with the London County Council and local authorities for permission to use the school fire stations as production workshops, so that when the raids became less frequent there was no idling around during "All Clears". Each station elected a production committee which in turn elected a production manager, who would travel the local factories for work to be farmed out to the stations. The station personnel were taught what to do, and during the evenings or after all station routine was completed they would go into production. A record was kept of each person's work contribution, and pay was made according to the rate fixed between the Union and the firms concerned. Many people came in during their off-duty periods to carry on with the work.

Plesseys, a big firm which made radio sets for aviation, was one of the biggest "farmers-out" in our area. Walk into a school fire station any day or night, and you would see the personnel, men and women, hard at work soldering and wiring radio sets. In schools where there was no room for production the members of the fire service would volunteer for work in the local factories, timber yards and wharves on their off days.

The National Fire Service offered to set up two Commando

divisions to be trained to serve with the troops on the Second Front. I volunteered and was drafted with others to Chigwell where with the R.A.F. underwent Commando training. I was posted to No. 1 of the two divisions to be sent to Europe after the landing of the troops. But I never got there, because in the end the Army required only one division; the choice was determined on the toss of a coin by the Divisional Commander, and our division lost.

7

Graduation—to the Port of London

It is 1945. The war is over. The Nazi war machine and its military might lies smashed and broken on the Eastern and Western fronts of Europe, defeated by the tremendous courage of the allied armies, the guerrilla and partisan underground forces and the civil populations. With the defeat of the Japanese armies in the Far East, with Mussolini hanged upside down and Hitler swallowing his cyanide pill in the underground shelter in Berlin, world fascism was smashed, democracy had triumphed and peace, peace at last lay before us.

The common people all over the world, who had suffered the most appalling hardships, dwarfing all previous inhumanities in the history of wars and human conflict, heaved a deep sigh of physical and spiritual relief, dried their aching eyes—if they had any tears left to dry—and gathered their weary limbs to start rebuilding what had been destroyed. But first, to welcome home their dear ones—fathers, sons, husbands, daughters from the far-flung theatres of war all over the world. Flags of welcome streamed across the streets. Over the doors of the fortunate hung the words: "Welcome home, Dad—or son Bill, or daughter Janet or Mary."

Bonfires were lit in the streets. Children who, during the nights of the blitz had courageously kicked out the incendiary bombs dropped by the Luftwaffe, danced around holding the hand of a Dad, a brother or an uncle, a veteran from the Burma jungle or the 8th Army, a member of the Royal Navy or a silver-badged seaman from the Merchant Navy who had survived the perilous seas of Murmansk carrying arms, food and ammunition to the gallant Red Army—and with the other hand clasped the hand of the mother who, after working long hours on production, queuing up for rationed food, had come home night after night to wash them and get them ready for the Anderson shelter or the nearest deep Underground. (These underground shelters, in the East End at any rate, had been wrested open for the people by the action of the well-loved Communist Councillor Phil Piratin who, during a very heavy "Blitz" had marched the people down Aldgate to the underground station. Other boroughs followed suit and the authorities were forced to make provision for the people to sleep there.) There the mothers would put their children to "bed" and lie down with them, waking in the early dawn to take the kids home, wash them, give them their breakfast and get them ready for school—then go off for another toiling day in the factory, too fatigued to listen to *Music While you Work* or *Workers' Playtime*. What wonderful mothers they were! and at last here they were, some with deep grief for the absent ones, but happy for the moment, united with families and neighbours, dancing, singing, kissing and hugging until the early hours of the morning. And again the next night . . . and the next . . . but reality soon took control again, and preparation for the new tomorrow had to begin.

Demobilisation of course affected the National Fire Service. Those who had been in regular employment prior to the war made application for an early release from the service, but those—like myself—who had no job to go to, were given the opportunity to stay on if they wished. While I was debating whether to stay as a fireman or return to the building trade, my wife's uncle, who was a registered dock-worker, told us that the National Dock Labour Corporation (a war-time body) was engaging non-registered men as an interim measure while awaiting the return of registered men from the Forces. I had had my own youthful, romantic ideas about the sea and ships, and had tried without success to join the Royal Navy. I decided that the nearest I'd ever get to fulfilling my boyhood dreams was to work on ships, even if I could not sail on them. I applied for my release from the Fire Service, and made application to the National Dock Labour Corporation. I was accepted, and in June 1945 I entered my University—the Port of London.

The "ology" I was to study was "dockology", and after working twenty-two years on ship and quay, and having taken an active part in every major strike in the post-war period, I am still learning. In my University there are no degrees or letters after

your name—except the remarks made by your fellow port workers
when they hear your name mentioned, and they have very long
memories.

And so, dear reader and friend, if you will be patient I will try
and hold your interest to the last page with a brief story of the
docks and those who have served and still serve in one of the main
arteries of Britain's industrial life-line. A world of its own, which
still, in this atomic age of moon-probes for a landing by 1970,
has one foot in the Dickensian world of antiquated working
methods and last-century social and hygienic amenities, with
many human characters who could easily be identified with
those Dickens wrote about.

I set off for Ibex House in the Minories, with a letter from the
National Dock Labour Corporation and my membership card
of the Transport & General Workers' Union, Dock Trade Group,
which in due course were presented and examined. I was handed my
Dock registration work book and pay book. My registration book
was numbered Sector 6, which is the London dock area—the
short sea trade, mainly Continental routes. The Port of London
is divided into nine Sectors, and a registered port worker can
seek work only in the Sector to which he is allocated; before the
war a man could try for work anywhere he chose. As I left Ibex
House I suddenly became aware that the building seemed
familiar, and after a moment's scrutiny I realised that I had
worked on it during its construction before the war. I'd worked
for a sub-contractor, floor-laying, and had been sacked for trade
union activities. Now I had just left its inner precincts with a job
that depended on my *having* a union card. Ah well, life's full of
contradictions.

I was to start work on Monday. I spent an unsettled weekend,
with a Sunday night of broken sleep, worrying about my new
occupation and whether I should fit in without appearing too
much of a greenhorn. In the morning I presented myself for work
at Butchers' Row, close to Ratcliffe Cross—a place from which
famous navigators departed in former years of our maritime
history. As I approached, I found groups of men standing around,
smoking and talking, and overheard strange words and expressions—"greenacre", "piper" and "piper's pipes", "the stones",
"the slave". What to do next? Suddenly there was a kind of a
rush, and everyone lined up along the kerb, quiet and very attentive. From across the road came a group of individuals, one of

whom started to call out: "Charlie's gang! Bert's gang!"—and the next moment all I could see was arms, arms everywhere, with hands holding books and thrusting them into the hand of the chap who had called out. In less than five minutes I was the only one left "on the stones". "Give me your book, son!" said the chap who had called out. I did so. "Righto, son! You're *pro rata*!" I couldn't believe my ears—*pro rata*? What sort of a job was this, where you had to know and speak Latin?

Anyhow, it was apparent to everyone that I was "fresh caught" and they all got round me friendly. I was taken to a nearby coffee-shop for a cup of tea before starting. It was then that a tough-looking man, tall, lithe and sinewy, with an impish smile, a soft-toned voice and blue eyes came over and sat down beside me. The others address him, with respect, as Joe, and his surname was Doyle. He began to ask me friendly questions, telling me not to worry and that he would take care of me—which he did, with great skill and kindness.

When we left the coffee-shop I was taken to the quayside, where I clambered into a boat and was rowed out to a ship on the "fairway"—the term for the middle of the Thames where the ship was anchored. The boat pulled alongside, and men began to climb the "Jacob"—the ship's rope-ladder which dangled down the side. My new-found friend Joe made me wait till last but one and then gave me the O.K. nod. This was my first experience of climbing a rope-ladder—very different from a builder's ladder which always lays on the slant. I found it difficult to attune my body to the rhythmical movement of the rope-ladder, but Joe Doyle got on to it immediately behind me so that his weight steadied it and made it easier to climb.

Joe followed me on deck and then explained what my job was to be. I had to operate the rope attached to the derrick arm, driven by a steam winch, which would lift the cargo into the hold of the ship and lower the load into the craft—in most cases a barge—which would then be stowed by dockers waiting in the barge. As the winch raised the empty cargo load-net level with the ship's deck, it was my job to haul in the guy-rope attached to the derrick arm until she was centre of the hold, ready for loading again.

I was extra to the basic gang-manning of thirteen required for what was called overside working; the guy-man was termed *pro rata* (so that was it!) to the gang, whose piecework rate of output tonnage was divided thirteen ways. The *pro-rata* man's wages were paid separately from those of the gang but were equal to the amount paid to each of the members. When that part of the operation which required a *pro rata* man was finished; he would be paid off. But the basic gang *would remain until the ship or quay operation was completed.* This was known as the "Continuity Rule" introduced into the Dock Labour Corporation scheme during the war.

Prior to 1940, and the setting up of the war-time scheme of dock employment under the National Dock Labour Corporation, the employers could pay a man off at any time after four hours. This enabled the employers, through their foremen or labour superintendents, to play ducks and drakes with a man's livelihood, paying him off at whim (but especially if the man were an active trade unionist who demanded strict observation of all the safety rules agreed between the Union and the employers).

But the introduction of the Continuity Rule guaranteed that once you had begun work on a job, whether on a ship or in a quayside gang, loading exports or discharging imports, it was your job whether it lasted a day or x number of days, and under no pretext could the employer dismiss you. Should the work have to be discontinued for reasons outside the employers' control, you either returned to the Pool of reserve labour, to be allocated elsewhere if work was available, or received your "fall-back" guaranteed pay. When the work was resumed and the employer was ready to engage labour, he would first have to ask for the previous gangs; this was known as a "Re-call Job". Only if the gangs were not available at the time of the Re-call could he engage fresh labour.

This limited degree of job security, won as a result of years of struggle between master and man, the Continuity Rule, has been regarded by Britain's registered port workers from its inception right up to the present day, as their most treasured possession. They will guard it with the same intent and purpose as the Guards Brigade give to the Crown Jewels in the Tower of London, to keep it save from the thieving hands of the employers who would dearly like to take it from them.

The ship was finished, and so was my first job and first experience in dockland. I was handed my registration book, and took my farewell of Joe Doyle, who had nursed me through my novitiate. With a humorous glint in his eyes he counselled me:

"Well, there you are, son, you're a docker now. So take a bit of advice from an old 'un. Let your eyes be your guide, and your money the last thing you part with!" And, having discovered through our conversaton that I was a keen trade unionist, he added: "And remember, the blokes who shout the loudest aren't always the militant trade unionists they'd like you to think them." I was to experience this many times in the years ahead, and his words have often come to my mind.

I had entered the industry at a time when it was engaged in a bitter struggle with the employers for more pay and fringe bene-fits. The claim was for 25s. a day (the actual daily rate at the time of the issue was 16s.), increased piecework rates, guaranteed public holidays, annual leave, pensions, canteens, new toilets and medical centres. It was known as the Dockers' Charter. A militant port workers' committee had been set up, supported by the northern ports of Liverpool and Hull. Pressure was being put on the trade union Executive, but a Labour Government had been elected with the highest recorded vote of any political party in our election history. Naturally, the lads who had returned and were still returning from the various theatres of war, having experienced tremendous hardships and sacrifices, were determined to change the old order and the pre-war con-ditions of employment, and to build a new life, with better living standards for their families, and dignity in their labour. They were prepared to fight the ship-owners, the stevedoring contrac-tors and wharfingers—the most hard-bitten and avaricious of Britain's industrialists.

What was the reaction of the Labour Cabinet, the T.U.C. and the right-wing union officials? Out they came with a phrase which by now (1967) has become a cliché: "Don't embarrass the Labour Government!"—poncing on the loyalty of the working class and determined on no account to embarrass the purse-strings of big business.

However, they were to learn a simple lesson: that you cannot expect men to return to civilian life like a lot of docile kittens and puppies. These were human beings who had fought in the jungles of Burma and Malaya, with the First and Eighth Armies; besides learning the art of war they had become highly skilled in tactics—and now the time had come to use that skill in the battle for a better livelihood for themselves and their children. All this crap about being loyal to the government and the poor dear public fell on deaf ears: a man's first loyalty is to Mum and Dad, to the wife and kids, and they're part of the general public too.

So they used tactics: not a strike, but a work-to-a-day-work rule, no piecework and no overtime. This was a terrible blow to the shipping and docks employers, an unpardonable sin in their eyes to refuse piecework and demand the implementation of the safeguards laid by the Board of Trade and Factory Acts. It meant that production was slowed up, and the employers were paying wages to 80,000 registered port workers (that was the strength of the National Register at that period). The result was a huge slice cut from their profits, and neither they nor the union executives could do a thing about it.

The campaign began to build up from port to port. I, incidentally, had been elected a member of the unofficial Port Workers' Committee of Sector 6, London Docks. It went on for three weeks, in spite of the usual vitriolic and distorted attacks made against us in the national daily newspapers—and in 1945 there was quite a number of them, champions of democracy and free enterprise. (Where are they today? Swallowed up, most of them, by their more powerful competitors in the free-enterprise jungle). The employers, who had been biting their nails up to their elbows, could contain their avaricious feelings no longer. On the Friday of the third week they sent instructions to their ships' foremen to cut off the steam power of the winches and the electric power of the quayside cranes, and we were unable to continue working. On the Monday morning when we shaped on "the stones" to offer ourselves for employment, we were told that unless we engaged for piecework we would not be employed. This we refused to do, and 27,000 registered London port workers were locked out.

Now at that time there existed a piece of war-time legislation for industry. In order to bring about the defeat of the enemy and bring the war to a speedy and victorious conclusion, a Clause had been inserted in the Statute making strikes and lockouts illegal. It was known as Clause 1305, and any infringement of it by either side—employee *or* employer—carried a penalty of imprisonment. This had been supported by the trade unions, for the last thing we wanted was to hold up the war effort or hinder production, and throughout the war years, with the exception of very minor incidents, this Clause 1305 had been honoured.

So here we were, in 1945, locked out by the employers, with Clause 1305 still in operation—and the Cabinet and the right-wing trade union officials, for all their pious statements about loyalty, never moved a finger to invoke it against the employers.

But as I said earlier, the workers who had stood together with our allies of other lands to defeat the most vicious war machine in military history were not to be broken by the smart-Aleck tricks of the employers. We stood firm. Finally it was the employers and trade union executives that yielded to our determination. Negotiations were opened between the employers and the unions which resulted in a victory for the port workers of Britain. Although we did not achieve all our demands, we did gain a wage increase of 3s. a day, bringing daily time-rate from 16s. to 19s., with a proportionate increase in the piece-work rate, both to be paid retrospectively. This was, at the time, the highest wage increase ever obtained in the history of our industry. We returned to work jubilant and victorious, determined to maintain the inter-port unity that had been built up through the National Portworkers' Unofficial Committee, not to usurp the power of our accredited trade unions but to make sure that the demands of the rank and file members were acknowledged and acted on. (Clause 1305 remained—but more of that later on.)

This was the big lesson of the 1945 wage struggle, the first of the post-war struggles on Britain's waterfronts—that militant inter-port unity, coupled with continuous rank and file agitation, explaining the issues and relating them to living experience, emphasising the importance of the workers and their right to labour with dignity for themselves and their families, strengthened their pride in themselves and their resolute determination to force a proper acknowledgment of their role from the employers, the Government and the trade union officials. Tribute should be paid to the leadership and back-room boys of the National Portworkers' Committee (unofficial). Most of them, due to nature and the passage of time, are no longer playing an active role today.

In 1947 Britain experienced the coldest and most bitter winter of the century; the thaw did not come until May. Although war time rationing was easing a bit, it was still with us. The country was gripped by blizzards from Land's End to John o' Groats; old people were suffering a heavy death-rate from having to sleep in freezing rooms; coal and fuel were in short supply;

Britain—an island of coal in the ocean—was forced to import coal!

In dockland, the cranes were frozen. Fires were kept burning beneath them to melt the ice from the wheels so that they could be moved alongside the ships' holds for loading and discharging. It was during this time that I heard one day of an amusing incident. A particular gang was discharging a ship from one of the Latin American republics. In the process of loading the cargo-net they noticed a large hamper addressed to the Right Hon. Ernest Bevin, Foreign Secretary and former General Secretary of the Transport & General Workers' Union. The lads were very cold. It was almost dinner time, and not only was food short (due to rationing), so was money; it was Wednesday and except for their homeward fares most of them were "skint"— broke, without money. They looked at the hamper with longing eyes. "What do you think, lads?" said a voice. "Do you reckon our Ernie would object to our satisfying the pangs of our hunger in these times of trial and tribulaton?" "I'm sure he wouldn't," said another voice, and a third added: "One thing about our Ernie, he was a good trade unionist and the word Brother really meant something to him. Remember the time he took a docker's dinner before a wages tribunal?" By now the hamper had halted its journey towards the cargo-net and, going into reverse better than any super-car, had moved towards the wing (the side of the hold). There it was rapidly unfastened, revealing its contents: tinned turkey, ham, bottles of wine, cigarettes and cigars, with a Christmas greeting from the foreign government concerned. To provide an appropriate setting a packing-case was covered with a tablecloth made from the *Daily Herald* and the *Daily Worker* and a feast equal in splendour to that of Belshazzar ensued. The British Foreign Secretary, former champion of the dockers, was never, I am sure, more sincerely toasted than he was that day in Latin American wine. "Up the Workers!" "Workers of the World, Unite!"—I am sure Ernie Bevin would have joined in himself if he'd been present.

When the repast was over, it was suggested, I am told, that the job should be done clean. The empty wine bottles were put back, the carcase of the bird returned to its tin cleaner than a suit cleaned by Lush & Cooks, the empty cigarette cartons were packed all nice and tidy, and a piece of white board was made into a Christmas card with words of greeting and good cheer:

"Dear Ernie, wishing you a Merry Christmas, from Some of Your Own." I feel sure that when Ernest Bevin opened that hamper his working-class roots came to the fore and made him forget the whole affair; at all events no report seems to have been made to the Port of London police.

We were now living on the waterfront of Stepney, in Cable Street—the longest street in the East End. It begins about 500 yards from where the Regents Canal joins the Thames, that part that is charted as Limehouse Reach; it winds through the parish of Shadwell and ends at the London Dock, Leman Street. With the exception of the East India and Commercial Roads, it is the busiest thoroughfare in East London, with dock transport hustling through continuously. (At that time it had two lanes of traffic; now it is one-way.)

The house we had moved into was situated at what was commonly called the "respectable end", the reason for this term being that that part of Cable Street was not multi-racial and the pubs were not so much frequented by the crews of the short-sea-trading boats, the prostitutes and pimps, the flotsam and jetsam of waterfronts the world over, as those further along. And yet, apart from an occasional drunken brawl which now and then ended up in a knifing—out of which the national press made headline sensationalism—no part of Cable Street nor the area lying close to it could be regarded as Sodom and Gomorrah. Its residents were—and are today—decent, hard-working people, equal to those in any other part of London, North, South, East or West. In the streets and parks you can watch the toddlers, brown, black and white, all playing together with one common understanding—that they are children. It is only when they reach the end of adolescence that they come under the adult influence of racialism and its poison and begin to use de-humanising labels like "wog", "coon" and "spade". What a tragic thing it is that the healthy, natural sense of human brotherhood should get pushed further and further back as they enter the industrial world of commerce and profit, and sometimes disappear completely under the fierce economic pressure that exists there!

Our new home had six rooms, a back garden, basement kitchen and scullery. Because the previous occupant had been an inspector for the Metropolitan Gas Board, he had refused out of loyalty to his company to have anything to do with electricity, and even his radio had worked by battery and accumulator. Consequently, until the Tory government removed the Rent Control Act (with no fight back from the Labour opposition) the rent was fairly reasonable. The house had been built about a century ago—with the class approach prevailing at that time. The gas and water pipes entered from the road mains through the wall of our basement kitchen, ran along the fireplace wall close to the ceiling and through into the scullery, where one fed the cooker and one the kitchen sink; the sink drained away into a trap to the sewer below the basement floor. Time and time again we found that this had been removed by the sewer rats, until I eventually approached the Council and the Water Board, who ordered a different system: this was to seal the sewer trap and re-direct the waste to the outside garden sump which was situated near the lavatory—and what a palatial affair that was! Its door had a two-foot gap top and bottom, and as you sat there meditating you could look up and see the sun in the morning and the stars at night; it came to be said in our family that you were going to the "Hill Billy".

The part of Cable Street where our house stood used to remind me of the French novel *Clochemerle*. On the opposite corner there was a public, ground-level Gents' Convenience, right next to the Children's Hospital; facing it was an undertaker's shop; to the right of it an Anglo-Catholic Church, then a pub, and on the other corner there was a butcher's shop—all within twenty yards of the convenience. In the summer after visiting it, the flies could take their choice of the children's hospital or the butcher's. How long would this situation have been tolerated in the Royal Borough of Kensington or Westminster?

It was in 1947 that we learned that a number of our older members were about to be sacked under a new label. Not redundancy—"inefficiency"—their crime being that they had failed to make sufficient proving attendances for work. The employers, who are represented on the London Dock Labour Board, sharing control with the accredited trade unions, were demanding their removal from the Register. Agreement had been reached by both sides, and the old lads had received their letters notifying them of the Board's decision. They came down to the Sector and contacted Wally Jones, Chairman of the unofficial London Port Workers' Committee.

Now Wally was a big, tough-framed man with a tremendous

pride in our industry and those who toiled in it. When he read the brutal letter of dismissal, he got angry. The rest of the committee were equally incensed. A mass meeting was called, where the recommendation to stop work until the old lads were reinstated was unanimously adopted. Sector 4, with 9,000 men, was at a complete standstill within a couple of hours.

Now the official union tortoise moved into action. Stratford Town Hall was hired for a mass meeting, where the men were to listen to the reasons for the sackings. The officials were confident that once these had been heard a return to work would be agreed.

It was a Friday evening. The atmosphere of the Hall was charged like a summer heatwave thunderstorm, packed tight and bubbling like a witches' cauldron. On the platform were all the union officials, paid and unpaid, and the Big Gun was the highest docks' official for London, Arthur Bird, a very capable orator who knew all the recognised jigs and reels for the pacification of the emotional rank and file.

The chairman opened the meeting: he was an ultra-constitutionalist and had worked during the official strike, and his introduction received a rough handling. But he was thick-skinned and carried on with the usual chairman's build-up before calling upon the Big Gun.

Up got Arthur Bird, National Dock Secretary, quite at ease and playing it cool. He had sensed that feeling was running high among his audience, so he started off quietly, recalling the days when he was young and the men of his time who had assisted him in his education and advised him to attend Ruskin College. Surely they had the confidence in his sincerity to believe that, based on the irrefutable evidence placed before the Board by the employers, the Board could take no other decision than the one it had taken. He sensed that a change had begun to take place in the mood of the rank and file, reacting to his "I-am-one-of-you" gambit. Now was the time for the kill. Listen to this, lads, while I read out the records of our poor unfortunate brothers (real con. stuff!). Then he began to quote: "Bill Evans, medical evidence, based upon certificates, suffering from chronic arthritis, only twenty appearances in a year. George Atkins, asthma, thirty attendances. Joe Wilson, spinal trouble, eighteen attendances . . ." and so he continued, in a subdued tone of deep sympathy. The atmosphere grew less charged. Suspicions were on the wane. We militant activists had silently watched the qualitative change taking place, and so had Arthur. He got ready for his *coup de grace*, closing his speech in deep tones of reverence for the old chaps: "What other alternative was left for us, much as our hearts went out to them?"

With both hands raised in a plea, he sat down. As he did so, a figure strode down the gangway towards the stage, shouting: "Give them nine doctors each like the King has got, not the bleeding sack!"

He was Morris Foley, a member of the Foley clan who had a strong reputation in dockland for staunch trade unionism. He was referring to the headlines in that day's evening newspapers, that King George VI, who was suffering from thrombosis in his leg, was in bed with nine eminent physicians and surgeons in attendance.

Instantly the place was in an uproar. There were cries of "Keep out! Keep out! No return until they're reinstated. Vote with your feet!" Morris Foley's outburst had gone straight to our class feelings. We all poured out of the hall, as Arthur Bird sat slumped in his chair, slowly shaking his head.

The unofficial strike continued for about a week. Then the Establishment—the London Dock Board—decided to withdraw the notices of dismissal and reinstatement took place. Once again the determination of the rank and file had saved the day and defeated right-wing collaboration with the employers. Many of those old lads remained in the industry—to retire with £100 grant and the princely sum of 10s. a week after forty years' service and all the steel burned out of their bodies creating record profits for the shipowners and stevedoring companies.

From about that time to 1956 there existed in the Royal Group of Docks, Sector 4, a sort of industrial Socrates discussion forum. There were about seven of us who, during times of heavy unemployment, after proving attendance for work at the Sector office and getting none, would retire to a local coffee shop or, if the weather held good, to the local park. Heated discussions would then take place on subjects such as political economy, dialectical materialism, what was meant by qualitative change and quantitative change and in what order they appeared in the class struggles of a capitalist society. Those of us who were Communists were expected (or thought we ought) to know the right answers, but there was some very sharp intellect among the non-Party lads and we struck sparks off one another's minds to the benefit of all. Among the seven was a lad whom I regard as the nearest approach to what is called a "worker-intellectual" I've encountered in all my experience. He was short, slightly-built, sharp of tongue—at times quite vinegary and caustic, particularly with those he considered to be pseudo-militants, the armchair socialists. At one period of my maturing years I was very critical of him and summed him up unjustly. That was before I learned to assess and value people in balance. His name is Bobby Grimme, and at times he could be like his surname. Today I am pleased to call him a close friend. His mind is a store-house of English literature, and on many occasions in those days he would contribute to our discussions the philosophy of Locke, Spenser, Hobbes and Nietzsche.

Then there was Sandy Powell, ex-professional wrestler, who had played a leading role on the 1945 Portworkers' Unofficial Committee, a good orator, very keen on biology and photography; in my opinion he would have done well in the teaching profession. Alfie Crocker, very skilful in the use of words, was always capable of turning the most simple argument into a dialectical discourse. Joe Cowley, a friend whose opinions on dock problems I value very highly, small of stature but of tough physique, cool and calculating but very quick-tempered especially against unprincipled men, was the one who always demanded the coming down to earth, the relating of everything to reality—I remember one morning in particular when we got on to Bishop Berkeley and the external world only existing in the mind. . . .

We talked about Art and the merits of different schools of painting, sculpture and architecture. I recall one afternoon during a strike when, after being relieved from our stint of picket duty, we adjourned to the nearest park to rest our feet and bask in the sun. Joe Cowley, ever restless, opened up a discussion on the purpose of art, with special emphasis on painting. Did painting and sculpture, like most material creations of early mankind, arise as something with a use value and then, with the centuries of development from primitive communism to capitalist society, lose its altruistic purpose? Early mankind, for example, created things for use—shoes and clothing to wear for protection and adornment, houses, for shelter, and food to eat; but today in a world of cartels and monopoly capitalism, everything has to serve the priority of profit. And art too, wasn't that in the same

E

boat? I supported the general view of those taking part in the discussion that all art began with altruistic purpose, but it would appear that the artist of today, painter or sculptor, first has to make a decision: how can I compete in a world of gimmickry and fad? And some go along with it, and turn out slabs of colour-gimmickry, or grotesque figures in bronze or stone that—if they were to turn into living humans—would be rushed to hospital for osteopathy or grafting treatment. I have seen and admired some of the works of Henry Moore, but in the grounds of our housing estate we have the sculptured figure of a sitting woman with a head completely out of proportion (though I admit it does have a gimmick, for the head appears to be looking in three directions at the same time!) I understand that the Greater London Council paid £7,000 for it. "Yes," I can hear the remark, "it sells, that's the importance." And that seems to me to bear out what we were saying in our discussion.

This, then, was the circle of work-friends that I matured with. And the Principal of a Grammar School, who was introduced to us by a former docker who had left the industry to become a teacher, told us that he had not experienced such a high level of discussion among his own teaching staff during the meal-breaks in the staff dining room.

8

International Brotherhood

There is an unwritten law in dockland, stemming from the pioneering days of building trade unionism and passing down from
one generation to another, from father to son, that you never do
anything to impair another man's strike. Honour the picket line.
In 1949 this high principle was upheld with firm determination
by London's port-workers at the cost of great hardship to themselves and their dependent families, and the spirit of international
trade union brotherhood reached a high peak.

It arose from a dispute between the Canadian Seamen's Union
and the Canadian shipowners, who were in protracted negotiation concerning the shipowners' demand to cut the crew-strength
of their vessels. When negotiations broke down the Executive of
the CSU cabled all its members on the high seas to put the
crews on strike regardless of the country or port.

Now at that time we portworkers in Britain were unaware of
the struggle that the Canadian seamen had been carrying on.
When the Canadian vessel *Beaver Brae* tied up on the south side
of Victoria Dock, the stevedores who had been standing by to
discharge her after she had been securely berthed and the ship's
landing gangway was in position, walked aboard and took up
their positions at whatever hatch they had been appointed to by
the boss stevedore or ship worker. But as they began to remove
the hatches, they were approached by the ship's official trade
union delegate, who explained the situation and made an appeal
for international trade union solidarity.

After all, it was only four years after the end of the second
world war when Canadian and British soldiers had fought side
by side to defeat the Nazi war machine, enemy of democracy and
trade unionism all over the world. So the Canadian crew were

told not to worry. The operation of removing the hatch covers was stopped and word was sent to the Stepney headquarters of the Amalgamated Stevedores' and Dockers' Union, a small but tightly knit union, the oldest on the River Thames, with a very militant history behind it, popularly known as the "Blue" Union. (I know the name sounds a bit ironical but it got this name because of the colour of the contribution card, which is blue while the cards of the Transport and General are white and it in turn is called the "White" Union.) Its General Secretary, known to the whole waterfront as "Dickie" Barrett, was deeply respected by his own members and by the docks trade group of the Transport and General Workers' Union who thought more of him than of their own General Secretary, the late Arthur Deakin. Dickie had come up from out of their own ranks and had served his time in ships' holds. Within an hour of being contacted, he was at the quayside discussing the whole situation with the Canadian shop steward, and to his everlasting credit, he instructed his members to replace the hatches, saying that he would handle the situation the following morning.

In the meantime, dockland's grape vine, the fastest in Britain, went to work. The dockers who were working in quayside gangs waiting to receive the discharged cargo from the *Beaver Brae* asked the local office of the Transport and General Workers' Union for instructions, but no clear cut decision was forthcoming. The following morning the air was charged with electricity. The employers were informed by the stevedores that they would work any other ship but not the *Beaver Brae*. The rank and file dockers, still without instructions from the Transport and General Workers' Union, acted on the advice of their unofficial committee, and made the same offer. The employers' reply was that all ships must be loaded or discharged or none at all. We refused to budge from our principles. The Canadian seamen's strike committee held a poster parade outside the dock gates appealing to us not to work the *Beaver Brae*. In trade union parlance, she was black. That was sufficient.

Every registered port worker, docker, stevedore and clerk attended the sector office to be directed to work, but the local office had received instructions from the National Dock Labour Board to carry out the employers' behest: "All or None." So there we were, not on strike, ready to work any ship but the *Beaver Brae*, but the employers and the Board were adamant.

So it became a lock-out—despite the fact that Clause 1305, the war-time legislation making strikes and lockouts illegal, was still in force. Not a peep was heard from the Labour Government's Minister of Labour at this wholly unlawful behaviour on the part of the employers.

Over at London's Surrey Dock, the sector which handles the bulk of the timber coming from Baltic or Scandinavian ports, the stevedores had taken the same line of action with regard to the Canadian ship *Argemont*. Down in the ports of Avonmouth and Bristol, our West Country brothers, under the lead of Joe Doody, also stood firm on principle though every effort was made by the authorities to intimidate and coerce them. The Transport and General Workers' Union officials pleaded for a secret ballot. Joe Doody and his committee confident of the men's determination, agreed. The secret ballot showed 646 in favour of strike action, 108 against. The officials nevertheless rejected the outcome of their own democratic procedure and had the audacity to declare the strike unofficial.

The effect of the Bristol lock-out now reached the northern port of Liverpool. A Canadian ship had been smuggled out of Avonmouth and was berthed in Liverpool for discharging. When the Liverpool lads discovered this, thirty-two men walked off the ship and declared her black; 1,500 supported the walk-off and threatened action against the Board if there were any attempt to suspend them. Eventually the figure on Merseyside grew to 9,500 and, regardless of the fact that the shipowners were in contravention of Clause 1305 (lock-outs illegal) the Prime Minister, Clement Attlee a *Labour* Prime Minister threatened the Mersey men with troops! (Troops were actually used down on the west coast to work on a banana vessel the S.S. *Baujano*.)

We were fortunate at that time to have two Communist Members of Parliament, Willie Gallacher and Phil Piratin who were asked to receive a deputation of dockers. With none of the usual waiting and kicking your heels in the lobby we were met by Phil Piratin who had arranged for a committee-room and contacted all the dockside M.P.s to receive us and listen to our case. We had come to urge the dockside M.P.s to demand the moving of the two strike-bound Canadian ships to berths in a backwater until such time as the Canadian seamen's dispute with their shipowners had been settled, so that we could return to work and the "national crisis" and the danger of food supplies running short—which the press was screaming about in daily scare head-lines—would not arise. Our proposed solution was simple and logical; all that was needed was a Cabinet decision to remove the ships in question and the nation's economy would be safe (not that it was in any danger—you'd think from the press that there were no such things as refrigerated warehouses, already chock full of meat and dairy produce).

We were listened to and questioned by the dockside M.P.s, who promised to do all they could. The following day, Phil Piratin, Willie Gallacher and others put questions in the House to George Isaacs, the Minister of Labour, but to no avail. The ships remained at their berths and we remained locked out.

But the struggle of the Canadian seamen and the solidarity of Britain's port workers had fired the imagination of the whole labour movement. Meetings and collections were held in mine and factory. Food parcels poured in from town and village. When a Government order was made on behalf of the Canadian shipowners that the seamen were no longer to be housed on board their respective ships two hundred homes were instantly opened to them and they were welcomed in as members of the family.

Saturday, June 25, 1949 brought a heart-stirring headline in the *Daily Worker*: CANADIAN SEAMEN'S VICTORY ENDS LOCKOUT. The shipowners had decided to reopen negotia-tions. The Canadian seamen's fifteen-week struggle had been victorious and it was a victory too for international trade union brotherhood. Seldom has that wonderful principle stood higher than in that eventful year of 1949.

Yet there were those who could not accept the fact that dockers were men of principle. Though we were now back at work Mr. Mellish a Labour M.P., declared in the House that somewhere along the line there must have been a Communist Plot (though I don't recall that the Communist Party had anything whatever to do with Clause 1305) and urged the Government to investi-gate—as if it hadn't been doing just that! After a number of weeks of thorough investigation, a government White Paper was issued. Its findings? As far as I know neither the Communist Party nor a single Communist was named. But Clause 1305 remained.

And there were further repercussions from our own Union. Six of us dock militants were brought before the Executive for an enquiry into our action in "unofficially" supporting the Canadian seamen. I shall never forget that morning at Transport House. We sat there like prisoners of the Inquisition, the General Secretary Arthur Deakin in the Chair and facing us the paid and lay officials of the Docks' Trade Group. We were questioned about our activities in the Canadian seamen's struggle and the dockers' lock-out. Veiled remarks were made about our membership (supposed or actual) of the Communist Party; a heated debate took place between Ted Dickens, Harry Constable and the General Secretary, with the General Secretary blowing his top. Finally, each one of us was asked in turn if we were prepared to carry out the Constitution of the Transport and General Workers' Union. Harry Constable replied: "How can you expect a straight yes or no? It would have to depend on the circumstances. To give an example: it's a punishable offence to break one of the Port of London by-laws. Now one of the P.L.A. by-laws says swimming in the dock is not allowed. Supposing I fall in the dock—do I obey the by-law and drown?" This was too much for Arthur Deakin, who again blew his top. Anyhow the result of the enquiry was that Harry Constable, Ted Dickens and Bert Saunders were expelled from the Union; Ted Kirby, Vic Marney and I were suspended for two years from holding office even if elected. (This didn't mean anything because a resolution had been passed at the Union's biennial Conference at Scarborough that year preventing members of the Communist Party from being elected to office whether as paid or lay officials—a double-edged attack on the democratic rights of all the members for it not only denied Communists the right everyone else enjoyed, to be elected, but deprived non-communists of the right to elect or propose someone they might consider capable of carrying out the duties of an official in the interests of the membership.) Tommy Cronin was merely admonished; within a short space of time he became a paid official and is now Chairman of the London Dock Labour Board. Strangely enough the other six of us were members of the Communist Party. . . .

For a while the port workers settled down to a peaceful lull, licking our wounds—for after all you can't go into an industrial struggle without getting hurt; there are financial problems, hire purchase arrears, borrowed money to pay back and the first week back you don't get any wages because the National Dock Labour Board keeps a week in hand. When I say "peaceful" it must be taken as relative; peaceful apart from the daily skirmishes between gangs and employers because of the nature of piecework and conditions.

For instance on a very hot day in July we were discharging rubber, which was in the form of cubes weighing about 4 cwt each—about four thousand of them all dressed with powder to prevent them from sticking together (though a lot of them were nevertheless stuck). It was a real back-breaking job and the piece-work rate was poor, as it still is today. The fact that a large per-centage of the cubes were stuck together meant that we could not work at peace-work speed. We called for the ship-worker (the equivalent of a factory foreman), drew his attention to the state of the cargo and asked him to contact his superior, the Labour Superintendent, and tell him that we wished to discuss a price for the job. This is custom and practice in dockland but the employers keep strict discipline; no single employer can pay the sum asked for, there must be an agreement by all the employers in the sector. In order to reach agreement on the job under discussion there must be a meeting of an area committee, consisting of representa-tives of the employers; meanwhile the local trade union officials discuss with the men the nature of the job how much is being asked and whether extra labour is required.

On this particular day the gang of which I was a member consisted of some of our most militant members, hard and fast principled men who, having made up their minds about what was required in terms of money and extra men, were not pre-pared to budge an inch from their demand. Any talk of a com-promise was as good as the proverbial red rag to a bull. At the appointed time, 10.30 a.m., the employers' representatives arrived at the ship and proceeded down to the hold to examine the nature of the job for themselves. Among them was a tough character, an ex-Naval Captain, well known to the men by the nickname 'Captain Odd-socks'. (This was because some years before as he was coming down the ladder into a ship's hold one of the stevedores, catching sight of his legs, had shouted out "Look! he's got odd socks on!" whereupon, red in the face, he had made a very profane remark and shot back up the ladder without even attempting to do whatever it was he had come down for.) When they were all down the hold, Captain Odd-socks had a go at shifting one of the blocks; having been fortunate enough to pick one that was not too badly stuck he succeeded after a few attempts in dislodging it, and turned to the rest with a sarcastic smirk, remarking "These aren't hard!"

Immediately there was a rejoinder from one of the gang: "No, not as f——ing hard as you!" The trade union official began to tut-tut. Tempers began to rise, and the men, whose backs and muscles were strained and aching from their hours of labour became very irate. An ugly scene began to develop. One of the labour superintendents admonished: "That's not the way to address your superiors!" Up spoke another member of the gang: "Mister, I don't like using clichés, but you can kiss my arse!"

The employers' representative retired to deliberate our demand with the trade union official. I, for one, did not feel hopeful, and we were all prepared to strike. But the other side must have sensed our mood, and after a long sitting they finally agreed to our demands.

You see, I hope, why I use the term "relatively" peaceful.

Yes, everything is peaceful on the waterfront, except for those of our members who get killed or maimed while trying to get a living at break-neck piece work of ten hourly stints for five days and four on a Saturday, and Sunday overtime of eight hours. In most cases it is a sixty-two-hour week, in spite of unemployment—no lead from trade union officialdom calling for a halt in overtime so as to share out the work. "We are very democratic. Only when our members call for action will we act. After all, it is their prerogative"—what mealy-mouthed unction they shoot off! The moment there is an "unofficial" strike that might extend outside its local confine, they are at the dock gate calling for a return, or issuing leaflets telling the men to take no notice of the "irresponsibles". Strangely enough, though many of the officers have served in the past on unofficial committees, the self-same men have sat on the London Dock Labour Board with the employers and agreed to suspend men who have taken part in a one-hour stoppage; which reminds me of the words of one of the great figures in English literature, Samuel Butler:

> What makes all doctrines plain and clear?
> About two hundred pounds a year.
> And that which was proved true before
> Prove false again? Two hundred more.*

---

*Hudibras

Words of wisdom that could be applied to many a trade union official, Member of Parliament and Cabinet Minister.

Still, there you are. We have all sorts in the dockland community too; the "characters"—comedians ever ready with their Cockney wit, who respond to every situation with a crack; fly-boys, with sidelines; betting boys; black sheep; the have-nots; men such as the one known as "the Wasp". Among working people, anyone who lends money and is not paid back says: "I've been stung". The day I encountered the Wasp for the first time, I happened to be working a Furness-Withy sugar boat. The top hand was a great, loveable character called Wally Jones, to whom I shall refer again. It was tea-break, and we were standing around drinking our tea on the ship's deck, when suddenly I could hear big Wally, in a warning tone, saying 'Zzz, zzz, zzz!" Others took up a second "Zzz, zzz, zzz!" and someone muttered: "Vanish!" Within seconds, the deck was clear, except for the two winch-drivers, who hadn't heard the warning buzz. We watched them through the window of the ship's gear-room. Before they could get the message, along came the Wasp, unfolding his story of misfortune. In deep silence, the winch-drivers' hands were withdrawn from their pockets, and each handed over a piece of silver. The Wasp, with a "Thanks, I'll pay you back Thursday", walked away to the next hatch, to try his hard-luck story again.

But we've also got men of high trade union principles, men who would give you their last penny, or every personal assistance in their power if they knew you were having it hard, so long as you were clean and not a "Tarry"—a term applied to anyone who worked during a strike, short for Tarry-leg, another term for blackleg.

I am going to digress for a moment about the stigma of being a "Tarry", the most unpardonable sin in dockland. When the Royal Docks Distress Fund (to which I am going to refer later) gave a farewell dinner to some of our old lads who were retiring at seventy-five years of age, I had the honour and privilege of acting as a steward and directing them to the tables and seats reserved in their names. It was a splendid affair. No money was spared, because we militant rank-and-filers had the deepest love and respect for our old 'uns, many of them fathers and grandfathers of men still working in dockland. We knew what hardships they had suffered at the hands of the shipowners, sub-contractors and wharfingers, when every little protective practice we, the sons, enjoy today, had to be torn from the employers at the cost of empty bellies, torn and broken limbs.

It was on this wonderful night that I realised how deep their memories went concerning "Tarries". I was about to show one old lad to his seat. He was very upright, smartly dressed and walking with dignity. Suddenly he stopped dead in his tracks.

"I ain't sitting next to him!" he said, pointing to an already-occupied seat. Naively I asked: "Why? Does he owe you money?" "Why?" he replied scathingly. "The dirty bastard was a 1912-er!"—which meant that the other old fellow had scabbed in the great strike of 1912. And this was now 1960!

That was, and still is, the character of the majority of London's portworkers: dockers, stevedores, lightermen and clerks, steel forged and tempered on the anvil of struggle in the class war. I am confident that so long as skill and industrial experience are passed down from one generation to another in Britain's ports, no employer or group of employers can break our determination for dignity and trade unionism.

9

Keeping Fit (and Pets)

Ever since boyhood, because of the fear of tuberculosis arising
from my childhood experiences, I have always been very health-
conscious and deeply interested in physical culture. Any opportunity I can get to sit, work or play in the sun, I seize on and strip;
at times I've been nicknamed "Nature Boy". Between the two
world wars, whenever trade union and political activity permitted,
I kept up physical training and weight-lifting at the local youth
clubs; and when I as in the National Fire Service I took a course
for physical training instructors which I completed with full
marks. In the early post-war years, I applied to the London
County Council's Physical Culture Education Board for an
appointment as an instructor visiting youth clubs and evening
institutes for two-hour sessions for which you were paid so much
per hour. After a day's work in the docks I would rush home, greet
the wife and daughter, take my evening meal, clean up and then
proceed to the Vallance Youth Club. This was situated in Commercial Street, in the crypt underneath Spitalfields Church,
opposite the fruit and vegetable market. It was, and is, a tough
area of squalid slums and narrow streets; in the churchyard you
frequently see the unfortunates, misfits and maladjusted members
of society sitting or lying on the benches—the "meths drinkers"
who have given way to despair. These are the surroundings in
which hard-working mums and dads have to rear their kids—
and if the kids don't get caught up in juvenile delinquency they're
lucky. It is an area where the local "vice squads" are busy, but
in most cases it is the victims who are arrested; the people who are
really responsible for the crime, misery and squalor are the
private landlords' syndicates and land property speculators who
charge astronomical rents for a type of dwelling that Prince
Philip, I'm sure, would not think fit for his polo ponies.

The club I chose to teach in was in this area. It was a challenge, but above everything else my pupils were working-class kids, children from decent working-class families, my kind of people. The Vallance Youth Club was ably managed by a local Labour Councillor named Michael Davis. A tiny man, who suffered badly from asthma, he was a giant in his endeavours to help the East End children, who lovingly referred to him as Mickey.

It was here that I met an extremely talented lad who lived in an old slum house down an alley off Swedenborg Square. He had no parents, lived in two rooms, and ate with the next-door family of Mrs Johnson, a widow with five youngsters. I formed a friendship with this lad, took him home and introduced him to my wife Ellen and my daughter Kathleen. They loved him. He became almost like a son, and when eventually he married he rented two rooms in our house. He had a burning desire to write. After working hard all day he would attend the evening institute to learn English and after a while he joined Unity Theatre, the progressive theatre that has given their first start to many people now famous in the theatre and cinema—Bill Owen, Lionel Bart, Alfie Bass, Joan Littlewood, Ted (now Lord) Willis and others. Anyhow, the lad's name is Michael Cahill, and when his TV play *Gracie* had its first showing on B.B.C. 1, my family and I sat there with pride.

Besides enjoying physical culture, I have a deep love of animals, especially horses and dogs. I couldn't afford a horse so it had to be dogs. I took up showing and breeding, and was introduced to a lovely breed—the Staffordshire bull-terrier, a great favourite in the mining district of Nottingham and in the Potteries. The Staffordshire is a very game breed, the oldest existing terrier bred in Britain, a pocket Hercules. And though it is illegal, there are still occasional contests held in secret at which bets are placed on the dogs. Apparently it is to one of the match rules for a Staffordshire bull-terrier contest that we owe the expression "Not up to scratch". A square having been marked out as the area of the fight, a line was scratched down the centre, and the owners of the competing dogs would toss a coin to decide whose dog should remain on the "scratch" while the other one was retired to a corner of the square. The loser's dog had to come "up to scratch" voluntarily, without any assistance from its owner and if after a number of "rounds" it failed to come up to the "scratch" it was declared the loser. It was very rare indeed for these game little dogs not to attempt to come "up to scratch", even if they had to drag their hind legs because they'd been so badly mauled. Thank goodness this sort of contest is illegal; they are such gentle, lovable dogs and especially good with children.

I had some success as a breeder and exhibitor and took a novices' First in the 1947 Southern Area Championship. But I didn't stay long in the show game, for in my personal experience it is a rat-race. You can have an excellent specimen dog or bitch, and if you are a small breeder of the back-yard or garden sort you will probably pick up plenty of novice-class firsts. But when you reach the end of the novice period and enter for the senior-class and championships against the established and famous kennels, the judging starts to veer in the direction of who is holding the lead rather than the entrant at the other end of it. I sold up and got out of it. But my love of dogs was too strong, and within a year I was back in. This time it was the Boxer breed. I never had sufficient money so I purchased a bitch puppy on breeding terms—that is, sharing the first litter that I bred. I don't know whether it was my cheek or the charms of my pretty daughter Kathleen who was with me at the time that persuaded the owner, a complete stranger, to let me have the puppy on those terms, but she decided in my favour, we made a bargain, I fulfilled the trust and a very firm friendship grew out of it. The owner was Mrs Barbara Williamson, wife of Mr Quintin Williamson, chief Forestry Commissioner of Britain's Southern Region. They are a lovable pair and in spite of our political differences we have maintained our friendship, for which I have a deep respect.

When Ellen and I moved into our present G.L.C. penthouse abode, I had to make the sad decision to have my Boxers put to sleep, for no pets other than goldfish or budgerigars are allowed there.

Friends sometimes ask me what I'd like to do when I retire. Well, I pipe-dream, like most working people, of winning the Pools (which I don't do), retiring to the country, breeding dogs, painting, going for long walks—and systematically visiting all the centres of London culture to contemplate and try to understand all the creative works of art created by man, for in my forty-five years of working to maintain enough wages for a decent livelihood for my family, there's been little time for this in my leisure moments.

One of the things I look for in the socialist society of the future that I'm striving for is a shorter working day and week (without pay cuts) which will give working people time to "stand and stare" and teach them how to use their leisure. You take the Festival Hall on London's South Bank, built for the 1951 Festival of Britain, with its breathtaking inner architecture and pure high-fidelity acoustics. Every time I visit it I enter with pride, conscious that this beautiful hall was built by my class— technicians, skilled artisans, bricklayers, carpenters, iron-benders, electricians, plasterers, painters and labourers from the four corners of the British Isles. When it was under construction you could hear brogues and dialects from every corner of the land; I know, because I visited the site during one of the London dock strikes to make an appeal for funds and solidarity—and got both. Yet throughout the years that have passed since then, I venture to state that the percentage of wage-workers attending to enjoy the concerts is like a spit in the Thames that flows beside the hall, the great majority coming from the higher salaried groups who have been *taught* (just as our lot could be taught if they had the opportunity) how to understand and appreciate the arts.

10

The Seven

In 1951 the becalmed surface of Britain's waterfronts began to show signs of a rising storm. Up on Merseyside, tempers were on edge as a result of a spit-in-the-eye wage increase that had just been negotiated by the accredited dock trade unions, with the late General Secretary of the Transport and General Workers' Union, Arthur Deakin, as principal negotiator. The spit-in-the-eye raise was the princely sum of 1s. 6d. a day; it had been accepted by the National Delegate Conference, but the rank and file of the Mersey were up in arms and not in accord with their delegates.

Within a few days of the announcement of the award, the London Unofficial Portworkers' Committee received telephone calls from the Merseyside Unofficial Committee in Liverpool, stating that the situation there was untenable and their rank and file were about to vote with their feet and walk out in protest. A further telephone call informed us that this had happened; 3,000 men had come out on strike against the accepted increase and members of the Merseyside committee would be arriving next day to make an appeal for unity from the London men—a unity which had been forged in the post-war struggles and reaffirmed at the formation of the National Portworkers' Committee.

The London committee agreed to meet meanwhile and discuss the Liverpool appeal. Under the chairmanship of the late Wally Jones, one of the finest of London's militants, sat some of the shrewdest and most experienced men in London's waterfront: Ted Dickens, the man with whom the employers had refused to sit and had asked for his removal from official union committees (and obtained it); Joe Cowley, ex-stevedore, now docker, with his cool, intelligent reasoning; Harry Watson, lighterman, deeply respected for his dedicated service in the best interests of the portworkers, excitable but very militant; the late Albert Timothy, and one of dockland's finest orators, Harry Constable. There were others too whose names I cannot recall, but who were equal to these in their integrity and their loyalty to the men who had elected them.

Now, the situation in London was somewhat complicated. A lot of water had flowed through dockland since the previous struggles of 1945, '47 and '49. The London employers had taken note of their experience of the post-war struggles, and had decided that the best way to further their interests was to create a sharp division among the port's registered men. No doubt about it, the lesson taught in Gibbon's *Decline and Fall of the Roman Empire* and drummed into every public schoolboy—"divide and rule"—had been well learned. Their policy therefore was to create a deep schism within the Port of London. Certain individual firms were allowed to operate a system of employment that gave their weekly workers guarantees which were unobtainable by pool men registered with the National Dock Labour Board: they enjoyed a full basic weekly wage whether they worked a full week or not, choice of holidays, and other benefits. With regard to discipline, the weekly worker could not be dismissed from the industry but was returned to the reserve pool of the London Board.

The accredited port unions, instead of using this as a precedent to bring the conditions of the National Dock Labour Board up to the level of those of the shipping companies, sanctioned these weekly-worker agreements, thus allowing the employers to create a private scheme within a national body under dual control by employers and unions (so that they had it both ways). This scheme somewhat naturally attracted a large percentage of pool reserve men, and the "divide and rule" policy worked as intended. A deep bitterness grew up between pool men and weekly workers. (After years of continuous appeals for unity between "pool and perm" this division became less sharp.)

This, then, was the situation facing the unofficial committee of London on the night they met to deliberate on the call for unity. There was also the fact that you cannot hand back an accepted wage increase. However, after many hours of intense discussion, it was decided to call a mass meeting of the rank and file on the "fields"—the meeting ground of those days.

The meeting was attended by about 500 men—out of approxi-

F

mately 9,000 in Sector 4, the Royal Group of docks. The delegates
from the northern ports—now including Hull and Manchester—
made a strong and emotional appeal for national solidarity. The
chairman of the meeting, Wally Jones, called for a vote of support, which was carried unanimously. With 8,500 men still at
work, this was suicidal. But the die had been cast. The chairman
proposed a line of action that was without precedent in strike
activity. This was to march the men through the gate into the
docks and urge those remaining at work to put on the hatches
and join us in the struggle. The meeting agreed. With the committee in the lead, 500 striking port workers stormed the gates of
the citadel, past the police on duty, who stood there spellbound
and powerless to stop us. We marched along the dock quayside,
with the police pleading for us to halt. To no avail. We continued
our march, calling in friendly voices to those still working to come
and join us. As they made no response, reason and courtesy
gradually faded into the background and many of our lads began
to use four-letter invectives. Eventually, after miles of walking,
we gave up, resolving to make a fresh appeal the following
morning.

Meanwhile, the National Dock Labour Board decided to take
action. This, in their opinion, was a wonderful opportunity to
behead the militants without protest from the rank and file, so
they got prepared to give notices of dismissal if we did not return
to work. Strangely enough, their plans were thwarted by the
action of Sir Hartley Shawcross, attorney general for the government—a very ardent "socialist". He made a *faux pas*. On the evening of the first day, the unofficial port workers' committee was
meeting in a pub called the White Hart in the Borough of
Stepney. Suddenly, the doors of the committee room burst open
and in stepped five hefty six-footers. Up spoke the chairman: "I
don't know what sector you're from, but I've never seen you on
committee. Who are you?" "We are the Law", said one of them,
"and it's a pinch." "A pinch?" said Wally, "What on earth are
you talking about? We are a strike committee!" "That's it,"
said their spokesman. "We are arresting seven of your members
under Order 1305. Strikes and lockouts are illegal and you have
contravened the law."

The seven men were named: Ted Dickens, Joe Cowley, H.
Constable, Albert Timothy, J. Harrison, A. Crosby and F.
Johnson. They were led outside to a waiting Black Maria and

"THEY SHALL NOT PASS", ALDGATE 1937

TED DICKENS (*left*) AND JOE COWLEY AFTER THE TRIAL OF "THE SEVEN"

whisked away to Bow Street Police Station, where they were charged under a war-time measure that had been contravened by the employers during the 1945 go-slow and in 1949 during the Canadian seamen's strike without a peep of protest from the Labour cabinet.

However, Sir Hartley's action boomeranged, because where the unofficial port workers' committee had failed in its attempt to win mass support the arrest of the seven men did precisely the reverse. During the weekend, the whole of Britain read about the arrest in the national press, and heard it on radio and television. On the following Monday morning, 19,000 port workers walked out to a man, in protest against this attack on the rights of the individual and their trade union principles; and within forty-eight hours, the major ports of Britain were out solid.

A slogan was devised: "When They're in the Dock, We're out of the Dock!" Each time the seven appeared in the court-room dock, the whole of London, Liverpool, Hull and Manchester, with sections of the smaller ports, walked out of the shipping docks. A Defence of the Seven Campaign was set up. Printed cards were issued in the form of a receipt for a contribution of 2s. 6d.; these were headed "Appeal Fund for the Defence of Seven Dockers, charged under Order 1305, February 1951". Further down, in small print, they read: "This is to acknowledge receipt of 2s. 6d. to secure legal defence for our brothers and help secure the abolition of Order 1305. Signed, London Portworkers' Committee."

The response to this appeal was tremendous. Money poured in from all over Britain, from factories, mines, shipyards, rail and bus depots, building sites and from some official trade unions and universities. The demand for the release of the Seven was voiced by the whole of the British labour movement; the money raised enabled us, with the help of our solicitor Jack Gaster (who was and is a tower of strength to the trade union movement) to engage one of the finest legal members of the Labour Party, a consistent parliamentary champion of the cause of the common people, the late Sydney Silverman.

On the morning of the first appearance of the Seven in court at Bow Street, the Port of London was still and silent. We organised a march from the Temple underground station on the Embankment. Trainloads of dockers arrived at the station by underground, having marched through the ticket barrier telling the collector that "the bloke behind" had the tickets, shouting slogans meanwhile and carrying banners that had been hastily made overnight. The carriages were filled with demonstrators, and when we alighted at the Temple station we poured up the staircase singing songs of freedom such as *Land of Hope and Glory* ... I'm confident that Sir Edward Elgar would have been pleased with our rendering of his song, especially the emphasis we put on the line "Mother of the free."!

Sweeping past the ticket collector at the top, we formed up outside the station and marched off up the hill into Covent Garden, tangling up with the porters delivering fruit and vegetables to the greengrocers' lorries and carts. When they recognised us from our slogans and banners they sent up a chorus of cheers, and "Good luck, lads!" "We'll help if we're called on!"

Finally we reached Bow Street. Everyone wanted to get into the first hearing, but the court was too small to hold more than a few. The rest formed a queue outside, under the direction of the police. Feelings rose high when one of the committee, our popular Vic Marney, was arrested for "obstruction" and taken inside, but we calmed the lads down and an ugly incident was averted. During the long wait that ensued, balloons were blown up and sent floating into the air with slogans on them: "Release the Seven!" "1305 Must Go!"—to the accompaniment of loud cheers. An old "gin-biddy", well saturated, meanwhile moved around offering gin to the lads and singing to their great amusement. (Apparently she enjoyed herself, for she turned up on subsequent days and even on the day of the trial at the Old Bailey.)

The court hearing lasted two days. The Seven were sent for trial. As they emerged from the court, on bail, they were surrounded and chaired right through Covent Garden, to the tune of *John Brown's Body*. In the Strand they were put in taxis for home and the rest formed up. With a very good friend of mine, Johnnie Daniels, a militant ship's clerk and one of the shrewdest of men, I led them down Fleet Street, zig-zagging to and fro across the traffic, causing hold-ups and giving our police escort a very hectic time. It was pouring with rain. As we approached the *Daily Express* building, Johnnie and I conferred, and decided to march into the building and demand to see the paper's chief Industrial Reporter, Trevor Evans, who had been writing some particularly vitriolic statements about portworkers past and present.

We stormed through the glass portals of what was at that time considered the showpiece of Fleet Street newspaper offices, marched up to the reception desk and demanded to see Trevor Evans. A commissionaire came bustling over, all agitated and making remarks about bloody Communists. His remarks created a storm; a middle-aged stevedore made a grab at him with the remark: "Don't you call me a bloody Communist! I am *anti*!" We calmed our colleague. Meanwhile at the desk the phones had been busy, and we were informed that Trevor Evans would receive a deputation of three in his private office. Johnnie Daniels, Toby Mahoney and I were elected. Can you picture the scene—four hundred or so angry portworkers, soaked to the skin, taking a vote in the hall of that glossy glass house?

The three of us were taken up in a lift and shown into the private office of Trevor Evans. He greeted us a little apprehensively. We must have looked a tough trio for we were in an angry mood. However, after a few exchanges the atmosphere grew less tense, and the interview ended with a promise that Trevor Evans would always carry out a double check on statements emanating from sources outside of dockland. We shook hands and the three of us returned to the entrance hall, where I stood on a short flight of steps beside the lifts and gave the lads a report on our interview. We made a bit of history in Fleet Street that day.

The campaign grew in volume. Demands came from factories and building sites for us to send speakers. On one occasion I was invited to address the students at the London School of Economics, which I did, and was very well received. I have been back there many times in subsequent disputes.

The day of the trial arrived. Sydney Silverman had engaged a woman K.C., Rose Heilbron for the defence—I believe this was the first time a woman K.C. had appeared at the Old Bailey. Hours before the trial was due to open, thousands of dockers had arrived outside the Court. The neighbouring A.B.C. was packed with dockers, stevedores, lightermen and clerks having breakfast, while waitresses rushed up and down trying to satisfy their gargantuan appetites. As the hour of the trial approached, everybody moved out, and when our seven lads reached the portals a big cheer went up; there was a rush to shake their hands and pat them on the shoulders, with cries of "Good luck!" A further big welcome awaited Sydney Silverman, Rose Heilbron and Bessie Braddock, the Labour M.P. from Liverpool.

Thousands of us had to stand outside and await the outcome of the trial, bitter and angry that this should be happening under an elected Labour government. Hundreds of balloons were let go with the well-known slogans, "Release the Seven!" and "1305 Must Go!" painted on them. Building repairs were being carried out on a section of the Old Bailey, and some of our lads managed to write a slogan on the skip that was travelling up and down; each time the skip rose into the air with the words "1305 Must Go!" written on it in big letters, a big cheer went up from the waiting dockers. By now it was nearing opening time for the pubs and many of the lads were wetting their lips. (Our old friend the "gin-biddy" was there all right, but she didn't depend on opening and closing hours to get charged up.) Things seemed to be going very slowly, the lads were getting edgy and restless. So we decided to break into song. It's amazing what meaning you can put into such songs as *Rule Britannia*, *Sons of the Sea*, and *Land of Hope and Glory* if you're in the right combative mood, and there was a moving rendering of *Kevin Barry* from some of the Irishmen present. Now, I don't know if we were being too patriotic, or if we were disturbing the office staffs in the adjacent buildings, but quite suddenly, up from the direction of Snow Hill Police Station, our tuneful chants were interrupted by a clip-clop, clip-clop, and sure enough, there were the Cossacks—the mounted police—trotting towards us.

The patriotic singing took on a greater fervour and volume. With skilful horsemanship, the Cossacks began to manoeuvre us from the middle of the road to the pavement; then one over-zealous chap rode his horse into the pavement and hemmed a group of men against the wall. A police helmet went flying. Out came the batons, and it looked for a moment as if a major conflict was about to start. Meanwhile a young policeman noticed the old "gin-biddy" who had retreated for safety to the steps of a gents' toilet. He gave her a push; as she fell she grabbed the railings with both hands—and must have thought she was behind bars. She began to yell: "Let me out, let me out! I'm innocent!"

Law and order was precariously restored. We resumed our anxious watching of the Old Bailey. All of a sudden there was a rush down the steps, and the cry: "They're free! They're free!"

With cheers and shouts of joy, the crowd surged to welcome the seven freed men, who were immediately lifted shoulder-high. Sydney Silverman was chaired too and amid all the excitement Johnnie Daniels and I were rash enough to try and chair Bessie Braddock!

What a victory for dockland's militants! I feel extremely proud of the leadership given by the unofficial committee, but I deeply regret that the Transport and General Workers' Union did not lift a finger to free the Seven.

Well, there it was. Seven sincere, militant trade unionists saved from imprisonment, the British labour movement freed from the shackles of Order 1305 and the right of free men to withdraw their labour restored after eleven years. The most important post-war victory for the trade union movement—now betrayed by the Unholy Trinity, architects of the Prices and Incomes Policy (the great con) with its Part 4 legislation providing a fine of £500 for an attempt by the rank and file to maintain the same right. These three will be known as the men who put back the clock of industrial history by ninety years—for in 1872 two stokers at the Beckton Gas Works were jailed for a year under a Tory judge for the "crime" of striking for higher pay.

I I

"White", *"Blue"* and Unity

The London Docks' Liaison Committee is the continuation of the old Unofficial Portworkers' Committee, which was first formed in 1945. The change of name was the result of an official ban imposed by two of the oldest unions serving riverside and enclosed-dock workers, the National Amalgamated Stevedores' and Dockers' Union, and a very important old craft union, The Watermen's Lightermen's and Tugmen's Union—whose members have to serve an apprenticeship and compete, in their coming-out year, in the toughest boat race on the River Thames, known as *Doggett's Coat and Badge* (founded by Thomas Doggett in 1715).

The official ban was the result of an interpretation of an overtime clause in the Dock Labour Scheme; the clause stated that overtime should be worked "where reasonable", but the National Dock Labour Board interpreted this to mean that overtime was compulsory. Now, Fred Knight, a very capable and respected lay official of the "Blue Union" (the National Amalgamated Stevedores' and Dockers'—I have explained in Chapter 8 why it had this name) was told by the Labour Master of the Port of London Authority, the largest single employer in London, that he, Fred Knight, would be required to work overtime to 7 p.m.— two hours longer than the eight-hour day. Brother Fred Knight declined, on the grounds that he had to attend a trade union committee meeting that evening, begining at seven o'clock and it was therefore "unreasonable" for him to accept. He finished work at five p.m. The reaction of the Labour Master—what a title! It has the ring of the slave quarters of the Deep South— was that of a ruffled, pompous Dickensian beadle: he filed a complaint to the National Dock Labour Board under section so-and-so, clause so-and-so and Brother Fred Knight was sentenced to a day's suspension from work, with loss of pay. He appealed to a board, but the charge was upheld.

The executive committees of the "Blue Union" and the Watermen, Lightermen and Tugmen took an angry and bitter view of this. They held mass meetings—both unions are very democratic—and as a result a ban was placed on all overtime working until the Clause referring to "reasonable" overtime was removed. For who was to decide what was reasonable—the employer or the employee?

What was the attitude of the Transport and General Workers' Union in this matter? The committee of the National Dock Group adopted its usual right-wing attitude of collaboration with the employers, and refused to declare a ban on overtime in solidarity with its fellow trade unions serving the ports. But as usual they overlooked the role of the unofficial Portworkers' Committee and the strong support it enjoyed among rank and file members of the docks' section of the Transport Union. The unofficial committee convened mass meetings of the rank and file in support of the official policy of the two other unions. Consequently, the unofficial committee was always invited to sit in with the official executives of the other two unions in meetings convened to assess the progress of the campaign. From then on, the name was changed to "London Docks' Liaison Committee" and as such it is still known today.

The ban on overtime came at a very appropriate moment for, as a result of a "trade recession" (new labels for old wine—a slump in other words) there was mass unemployment in the Port of London. Despite this, overtime was still being worked: ten-hour stints, four hours on a Saturday, eight hours on a Sunday—a sixty-two-hour week in the midst of mass unemployment! The ban on overtime meant that the employers had to employ extra gangs for every ship's hold and quay-receiving gang. Overnight, unemployment practically disappeared and everyone was taking home a wage packet. It was one of the happiest of post-war periods.

However, it was not a happy period for the executive committee of the National Amalgamated Stevedores' and Dockers' Union, for the employers refused to negotiate on *any* question until the ban was lifted. But the majority of the 18,000 members of the "White" union (the Transport and General Workers') were supporting the official policy of the "Blue" union and the ban held firm. As a result of not being able to negotiate their members' problems, the National Amalgamated Stevedores' and Dockers' Union had no alternative but to call an official strike, to challenge the obduracy of the shipowners. In answer to the call of their Executive, 7,000 stevedores and dockers of the "Blue" Union walked out on Monday, October 4, 1954, in what was to develop into one of the bitterest of post-war strikes. It was a strike for principle—for the right of a worker to decide for himself whether he'll work overtime or not. The rank and file members of the Transport and General Workers' Union naturally refused to handle cargo that was normally handled by the stevedores and as a result of this, and of the arrogant employers' ordering of Indian seamen from the crew of the S.S. *Ghasan* to handle the baggage and cars for export, the Port of London was nearly at a standstill within a few days. By the end of the week, more than 11,000 Transport and General Workers' dockers had joined the 7,000 "Blue" union lads on strike. Dockers in other ports refused to touch the "black" cargoes of ships diverted from the Port of London. Dock trade union unity was once again restored, and so firm was that unity that the employers were to regret their provocation. Rank and file miners, engineers and other workers acted in sympathy, sending money to support the financial needs that a strike entails. On October 18th, more ports entered the struggle: 11,000 men in Liverpool and Birkenhead voted in favour of a solidarity strike with their London brothers. By October 20th, the number had grown to 38,000, over half of Britain's dock labour force.

Out came the press slanders—"Red Plot!" (how many times have we heard that scare!).

By October 21st the figure of men on strike had grown to 43,000. The Cabinet and the Minister of Labour, Sir Walter Monckton, were reported to be considering the use of troops, but they were fearful of the repercussions.

By October 30th, the London employers had caved in, though the national employers were still adamant—but with 44,500 portworkers on strike, victory was in sight.

At a mass meeting in London's Victoria Park, dockers, stevedores, clerks and lightermen massed shoulder to shoulder to hear their beloved "Dickie" Barrett announce the resumption of work on the following Monday morning. Victory was theirs. Never again could the dock employers threaten compulsory overtime. Dickie was followed by Vic Marney, popular Secretary of the unofficial Transport & General Workers' Union liaison committee. This was perhaps the greatest victory won by the united action of the portworkers for fifty years. Conscious that their fight involved a vital trade union principle, they kept their ranks without a break until the employers were forced to climb down. It had entailed sacrifices; but there was not a man who did not feel that the struggle had been more than worth while.

The broader labour movement had played its part in the struggle too. Its importance had been recognised, for had the most militant of industries been beaten, this would have given the green light to other employers. Throughout the struggle, delegates from the strike committee had been invited to speak at lunch-hour meetings at factories, building sites and shipyards, where generous collections were handed up from all trades.

It would be wrong not to mention the part the wives played in this struggle. Performing miracles of "making ends meet" on a non-existent family budget, finding part- or full-time work (where the family was not too large or too young for them to do so), pawning their cherished possessions—they stood solidly behind their menfolk. Women all over the country sent food parcels for the strikers' families. There's no doubt about it, the women will respond to a good cause every bit as strongly as the men.

Shortly after this, I received in my trade union branch a very pleasant surprise. Frank Lancely, our capable, competent and methodical branch secretary, read out an invitation from the Polish port-workers' union, sent through the auspices of the British-Polish Friendship Society, to send one of our members as part of a British trade union delegation attending the celebration of May 1st. The branch Chairman called for nominations. I was named and seconded. There were no further nominations. Lucky me! I was unanimously elected.

I got home from the trade union branch meeting very excited; there were two reasons for this—one, that I was to have the opportunity to study a socialist country at first hand; two, that I would travel outside of Britain for the first time in my life. However, I sat down to my supper and tried to behave as if everything were as usual. But Ellen, with that uncanny faculty of observation that wives have for their husbands' moods (par-

ticularly if they have been married a good while) allowed me to
carry on for about fifteen minutes and then said: "What's eating
you, love? Is there something on down at the docks?"

I'd had, I think, a slight feeling that Ellen might object,
for after all I should be absent from home for about sixteen days.
But she and my daughter Kathleen, who had just got home from
her youth club, were both excited and pleased for me. I kidded
a bit about not liking the idea of leaving them and having to
think it over and all that. But they were both too shrewd to be
conned, and within minutes we were all discussing it in a warm
family atmosphere. It never fails to amaze me, the unselfishness
of women.

It was in March that I got the news, and between then and
April 10th, the time dragged as if there were ten days to a week.
Ellen and Kathleen came to the airport to see me off to Warsaw;
we were all a bit anxious (there had been an air crash over the
previous weekend) and I was experiencing butterflies in the
stomach, never having flown before. I ordered two stiff rums
at the bar, and a brandy for each of my womenfolk and thus
fortified we made our farewells and I boarded the plane with
other members of the British delegation.

After an exchange of views with my neighbour, a young
Scottish engineer who was a member of the Labour Party, I
relaxed and started thinking how I should judge and assess
Poland. Should I do it by comparison with the standard of my
own country or with Poland's own past, present and future? I
decided on the latter, because here I was leaving a country that
was the first and oldest industrialised country in the world,
while Poland had been mainly agricultural, with very little
industry, particularly heavy industry, with feudal methods of
farming; it had been overrun by the most inhuman military force
in world history, Hitler's Nazi army; during the occupation three
million of its citizens (many of them Jewish) had been extermin-
ated in the horror camp of Auschwitz; all its major cities had
been devastated; two-thirds of its livestock had been slaughtered
or taken away to Germany—and I was making this visit only
nine years after the Polish people had started to rebuild from
ashes.

We landed at the airport just outside Warsaw. As the delegation left the plane were were met by three men and two women,
each holding a bunch of flowers. We shook hands, were greeted

with kisses and hugs, and each of us was given a *bouquet*. How thankful I felt, as I walked to the exit, that my fellow dock-workers weren't there to see me—I'd never have lived it down!

A great warm welcome awaited us at the hotel where we were to stay. We were introduced to the President and Chairman of the Polish Trade Union Council. The itinerary for our stay was read to us—and to other delegations from all over Europe—and we were asked if there were anything else we particularly wished to see. Arrangements had been made for visits to engineering factories, coal mines, collective farms, kindergartens and so forth, but nothing had been said about a visit to the ports. So I upped and asked, and though I was the only docker among all the foreign delegates, my request was granted.

If I were to write about all we saw, it would require a book by itself. But I must say a bit about my special privilege, the visit to the port of Gdynia. I toured the port with an interpreter who had served in the Polish Squadron of the Royal Air Force during the war; thus he spoke not merely *good* English, but English full of good working-class expressions, and we became firm friends.

I had free access to any ship I chose to visit, and exchanged information with ships' gangs concerning conditions of employment and payment, the structure of the trade union, and such questions as their right to withdraw their labour if no agreement could be reached between the port management and themselves. This last question caused a look of amusement all round. I was assured that the right to strike was guaranteed in the State Constitution. Had there been any need to use their right? Only on one occasion since 1945, I was told; and that had resulted in the official of the trade union's port committee and the port manager being removed as inefficient. How many hours of over-time, I asked, and is it voluntary? Nobody could work overtime unless sanctioned by the local trade union committee. Every port-worker was provided with a locker in which to place his street clothes, and was supplied with protective clothing free of charge; there were shower baths; regular medical examinations (and if their health was showing signs of impairment they were sent to a "preventorium" for six weeks on full pay; if at the end of six weeks there was no improvement they were transferred to hospital, still on full pay until recovery). A dock worker who chose to use the holiday facilities provided by the port enterprise was required to pay only 10 per cent of the cost for himself and his family, regardless of its size. I visited a training school for young port-workers who, having passed a medical test, were now on a course of tuition; at the end of the course they would do a day's work on ship and quay and then take a final written and oral examination before "graduating" to work.

Every care for the port-worker is strictly carried out. There is no unemployment. There are women crane-drivers—very efficient and on *equal pay*. I found that the conditions of the Polish port-workers were far superior to ours here in London—and that was in 1956.

During the whole of my visit I only experienced one sad day. That was the day we visited Auschwitz. At the entrance to the camp you see a great sign on top of the former headquarters: "4,000,000", written in huge figures—that was the total of those who died in this most brutal captivity, three million of them in the gas-chambers.

We were taken round by a woman guide who had herself been a prisoner there. Everything had been left exactly as it was when the prison-guards and staff fled at the approach of the Red Army. We were shown the gas-extermination quarter, which had been kept secret from every inmate; its orderlies were themselves prisoners, and were periodically executed in the gas chamber so that they should not reveal what went on there. We stood in front of the open furnace doors where a roller conveyor entered the oven; the barrows in which the dead were wheeled to the furnace were still in position. Under our feet was white ash—the ashes of the victims who had been incinerated after being gassed. This had all been built in the name of a "civilised" nation of Western Europe.

From there we were taken to two buildings. In one we saw huge piles—right up to the ceiling—of human hair, taken from the victims before they were put to death, to be sent back to Germany to make ersatz military blankets. In the other building were thousands of pairs of footwear, adults' and *children's*, false limbs, dentures and other possessions . . . that had belonged to living people. Tears streamed down many faces, including my own, as we looked. I shall never be able to forget it.

On the day before our return home, we were invited to the Polish broadcasting station in Warsaw, where we were given an opportunity to air our impressions, to ask questions and voice our criticisms "on the air". The general opinion of our delegation

was that Poland needed and wanted continuous world peace in
order to build socialism; there were gigantic shortcomings arising
out of tremendous obstacles, but in spite of this good advances
were being made because things were in the hands of the common people, working through their trade unions under the
leadership of the Polish Communist Party. I hope I can go back
some day and see how the progress has been continued.

12

Men of Dignity

In 1958, a tragic and sudden death befell one of dockland's most lovable leaders, Wally Jones, Chairman of the London Liaison Committee. Wally was one of those who grew up in Stepney, roaming the back streets and alleys of Wapping, playing truant from school to spend summer afternoons diving off Wapping stairs into the Thames, swimming round freighter barges, learning to fight and defend his person with bare knuckles. You had to be tough to survive in those tough back streets, unfriendly-looking wharves with narrow passages between them, down which many be-clubbed wayfarers had been carried by the press gangs in the old days to the waiting Merchant Navy ships.

With such a background throughout his childhood and adolescence, Wally soon learned that poverty and unemployment were not natural laws but built-in characteristics of capitalist society, and awareness of the class struggle was deeply embedded in his mind and all his activities. Wally was like a piece of well-seasoned English oak; big and rugged in physique, he was full of humour and loved a pint of good English ale. When you shook hands with him, it was as if your hand had been engulfed in a deep warm bucket. You could hardly see a pint glass when he held it in his hand. Woe betide anyone on the receiving end of that fist when it moved in anger!—which was very rare because Wally, like most big chaps, was slow to arose to physical ire.

Wally's industrial maturity was shown at its peak in 1951, during the Old Bailey trial of the Seven "unofficial" dock leaders. On their arrest he stepped in, re-formed the remnants of the committee and organised the defence campaign for their release, and for the repeal of Order 1305. Through his tireless activity, funds were raised to engage two fine lawyers, Jack Gaster for the London men and Sydney Silverman for those from the northern ports whose skilful fight helped bring about the release of the Seven and the removal of the anti-strike clause—one of the outstanding achievements secured by the rank and file militants of Britain's ports through unofficial action (while the "official" trade union executives remained mute).

Another aspect of Wally's character was that he was an extremely thorough and conscientious worker. Though the employers hated his principles, they had a deep respect for his working abilities. And it was this thoroughness that caused his death. On the tragic day in question he was the hatch-man—that is, the person responsible for giving hand-signals to the crane driver; the safety of the down-hold men lies in his hands. At one point he was standing in a position from which it was impossible to get proper view of a set of timber that was to be hoisted from the hold. In order to see clearly and be able to give the correct signals to the crane driver, he jumped onto that part of the hatch which was still covered—but one of the supporting beams was not secure, the hatch opened and Wally fell to the bottom of the hold and was killed instantly.

The Royal Group of docks in which he worked stopped work and went home. As the newly-elected Chairman of the Royal Docks Liaison Committee, I sought the chief of the Port of London Police and asked permission for his funeral cortège to pass in and out of the Royal Group main gates, so that the rank and file of Sector 4, the men he loved and who loved him, would be able to pay tribute to his passing. This had never been done before; nevertheless, permission was granted by the P.L.A. Police, and the Metropolitan Police Division of West Ham gave every assistance with traffic control, even to the extent of providing a motor-cycle police escort. A precedent was created. Since that sad day, two other well-loved and respected unofficial leaders have been paid the same tribute—famous veterans Albert Timothy and Ted Dickens.

No high official of dockland has ever been given such a farewell. It was the wish of the Liaison Committee to be Wally's bearers, and as we carried our beloved chairman from his home hundreds of his neighbours were there to pay him their last respects. When the procession reached the main entrance gates of the Royal Group of docks, the pavements were packed with dockers, the trade union brothers he had served so well; on "Speakers' Corner" where he had chaired so many meetings of

G

struggle against the employers stood two of the men for whom he had campaigned when they stood trial for fighting for trade union principles—Albert Timothy and Ted Dickens. As the hearse and mourning coaches entered the docks, hundreds of cranes stood still and silent, in upright salute. Slowly the procession moved round the police-box and out of the exit gate, while thousands of dock-hands stood bareheaded. Another veteran of the Old Bailey trial, Joe Cowley, solemnly placed on the coffin a wreath made in the shape of a cargo boat, then took his place in one of the waiting cars. Many tough faces were wet with tears.

Farewell, Wally. May I serve the men of dockland with the same sincerity of purpose, that London's port workers shall at last attain wages, pensions and benefits commensurate with their contribution to the nation's welfare, and the dignity of labour that is the birthright of every worker by hand or brain.

It was a beautiful summer day, a bit later in that same year, when I was on my way to a meeting of the Liaison Committee, to discuss the mass unemployment in the Port of London, which had reached the figure of 4,000 men reporting daily but unable to find a job. As usual, no lead was forthcoming from the National or London Docks' Group trade union executives; they seemed to have forgotten the unemployed members, though the unemployed pay the same contributions as the employed.

So here we are, a committee of five about to sacrifice our dinner time to try and work out some way to ease the situation. On my way to the meeting place, a back room in a coffee-shop (we have no fixed committee rooms) I bash into "Red Barrel Freddie", so called because of the amount of a certain type of ale he can put away. He is looking rather forlorn. I ask him what's bothering him, for he's usually cheerful. With a very dismal look, "Jack!" he says, "There are some pretty spiteful whoresons in this dock. Someone's sent a poison-pen letter to my wife, telling her that I've been seen *drinking milk* in a Fleet Street milk bar. I don't mind a bit of fun, but that's beyond a joke. Even my eldest boy believes it. When I left for work this morning he shouted after me: 'Ta-ra, Milky'!" Doubled up with laughter, I wished him good luck and left him using stronger invective than I've heard used against some scabs.

But things were serious. At the committee meeting we faced

the fact that a number of men were contemplating handing in their registration books; they were unable to continue week after week taking home what was left, after stoppages, of the fall-back wage of £7 8s. od. out of which money had to be found for fares, to report for work that was not forthcoming. A great number were experiencing serious hardship, particularly those who lived at a distance from the docks and might have to pay up to £3 os. od. a week in fares plus rents of £2 10s. od. to £3 os. od.

Men with twenty to thirty years in the industry were preparing to sack themselves. And what was our union's London Docks' Committee doing about it? Sweet F.A. So we five men, elected at dock gate meetings out of a personnel of approximately 9,000 men, sat trying to work out a policy. After keen discussion, we arrived at the decision that on the following Monday we would declare a ban on all overtime working. We were not happy with the situation, because we feared that the weekly workers—those men who were engaged on a private weekly basis with a single employer and therefore not facing continuous unemployment—would not support such a ban. But we ourselves, as a committee, and a large percentage of the pool men—termed casuals—were not happy to be working a sixty-two hour week while our less fortunate trade union brothers were getting no work. The proposal to ban overtime was put to the men at the Friday morning meeting and was unanimously agreed—but alas, the attendance was relatively poor, only a small proportion of the 9,000 labour force being present.

On the Monday morning we picketed the gates with posters appealing to our weekly-worker brothers to support the ban. By the evening the ban had won about a 60 per cent support. The committee decided to get in touch with other sectors of the port. The Liaison Committees of Sectors 5 and 6—the West India Dock and the London Dock—decided to support us. But unfortunately, because of the antagonism of the Docks' Group Committee of the "White" union, and the failure even of the "Blue" union executive to give a directive to the stevedore section of their organisation, the unofficial ban on overtime still had only partial results. Our committee decided to try for an all-out effort by convening a mass meeting at the Civic Theatre in the Borough of Poplar, the borough where the late George Lansbury lived and worked in the pioneering days of the labour movement.

The meeting was well attended. After the platform speakers

had outlined the urgency of the situation and made a strong appeal to trade union principle and the brotherhood of man, the meeting was thrown open to discussion. As this continued, for and against, I began to get the feeling that the men were disheartened at the lack of support from the weekly workers. However, the next speaker who came to the mike began a very strong, clear-cut appeal for unity of all sections of the Port of London. He illustrated his point by holding up a clenched fist, explaining that this was a symbol used by militant workers all over the world; then he opened his hand and showed how easy it would be to break each finger separately whereas once the fist became a united whole it was invincible. This had a profound effect on the meeting, particularly because the speaker, Harry Watson, was a very highly-esteemed man, a working lighterman and a member of the Executive of the Lightermen's and Tugmen's Union, well known to all.

The ban on overtime continued for another week. But because of the lack of majority support from the weekly men, our committee, the London Docks' Liaison Committee, had reluctantly to accept the situation and called dock gate meetings to end the ban. The number of unemployed continued to grow. Once again the official Docks' Group Committee had failed to give a lead and protect its unemployed members. I know of no other industry that would have allowed such a situation. In the building trade, when the site begins to reach an advanced stage of completion and the contractor starts to lay off men, the permit to work overtime is withdrawn by the Federation of Building Trades Operatives.

But in our industry, it seems that it is always the rank and file that is on the defensive, never the employers. Our negotiating bodies appear to approach the employers cap in hand, and the employers deal out as if they were handing largess from the Lord Mayor's Banqueting table. Talk about class collaboration! Why not argue from strength (as we are told we must do when negotiating with the Soviet bloc), why not use the same tactic when arguing for a wage increase, tell the employers that if they are not prepared to meet our demands the union will use the strength of its membership and call for a national withdrawal of labour? Such diplomats our negotiators fancy themselves, and yet they could go to a wage-negotiating conference and agree to a wage settlement that could not be divided over eleven work periods

without leaving an odd twopence—and had to call further negotiations a few days later to decide what to do with the odd twopence! (I'm not kidding! It was finally agreed to create a fund
for the benefit of the port workers and this was placed in trust
with the National Dock Labour Board until such time as it
grows large enough to dispense for the good of all.) When will
they come to realise that they have behind them a tough, militant
industrial army, ready to make sacrifices and face any hardships
for better living standards, for justice and the dignity of labour.

Yes, for the dignity of labour. I am going to step back for a
moment to 1954, to record a struggle for that very principle.
Though the men of the Port of London were not called on to par-
ticipate in this particular struggle, it warms me to record it
because its outcome not only gave dignity, it also proved that
Britain's registered port workers are not Luddite-minded about
the use of machinery. The struggle took place in the port of Hull,
in August 1954, and deserves a place in the archives of the
Trades Union Congress alongside the historic Match Girls' strike
in the 1889 battle for the "Dockers' Tanner".

The strike in Hull was to put an end to a method of discharging
grain-cargoes that had been in use since the time of the Pharaohs
in ancient Egypt. Imagine the scene if you can: a 10,000-ton
grain ship pulls in alongside of the quay. The gangway is lowered.
The waiting gangs of dockers climb aboard to discharge the
grain that is to feed the nation. It is 1954, the atomic age, the age
of speedy saloon cars, television, telephones, automation: and
in the ship's holds, gangs of four—two men holding open the
neck of a five-bushel sack and two men filling them with *hand-
scuttles*—are breaking their backs smothered with sweat and blinded
with choking dust, lifting fifteen scuttles to the bag, hour after
hour. Imagine unloading a 10,000-ton ship with a frying pan—
that's what it's like. After a few hours the men decided that they
had had their bellyful of these miserable back-breaking conditions and withdrew their labour, demanding that the vessel should
be mechanically discharged. An irresponsible action? Try it
yourself and see whether you think so.

At first the Transport & General Workers' Union officials
attempted to cold-shoulder the strike. But when they saw the
mood of the men, their attitude began to change. They called
a meeting of branch secretaries and chairmen (other members
of branch committees were not admitted) and after a two-hour

discussion it was decided to call a mass meeting to recommend that work should be resumed on all ships except the one from which the strike had started—the *Seaboard Enterprise*. But the Hull lads were firmly determined that dignity of labour should be acknowledged as theirs by human right. At one point in the struggle, because of the frustration felt by the men at the manner in which their trade union officials were handling the issue, there was talk of inviting the general secretary of the N.A.S.D., the stevedores' union, to discuss a mass transfer from the Transport union. But an appeal was made against this by Reg Spalding of the London liaison committee. (What a pity his advice was not taken; it would have saved years of splits, divisions and non-unionism in that port.) After eleven days of struggle, involving eighty-one ships and costing the employers £500,000, the strong, resolute Hull lads forced the employers to give in. "Unofficial" their action may have been; but the fighting militants of Hull won their battle for the dignity of labour and the use of modern methods.

However, in 1958, we London port workers experienced a different aspect of mechanisation; not a lightening of our labour but an attack on our manning-scales. It had been decided to introduce fork-lifting machinery into a Port of London Authority Department of Shipping, at 25–32 Sheds in the Royal Albert Dock, Sector 4. The rank and file were alarmed at the possibility of a reduction in gang-strengths. Branch 1/37, one of the most influential Transport & General Workers' branches in the Port of London, thereupon invited a leading docks' official, T. O'Leary, O.B.E., to attend and discuss the situation with the members.

The meeting was packed. The official launched off into a lot of statesman-like platitudes about how you can't stop progress, we were moving into the machine age and it was going to lighten our labour. It's amazing, the way officials can talk about mechanisation as *progress* without saying for whom, us or the employers. One of the members expressed this in downright terms. "It'll lighten our labour so much that there'll be no bleedin' labour to do, and we'll be redundant—is that what you call progress?"

This knocked the official out of his composure, and after a stormy meeting, Branch 1/37 went on record against the introduction of the fork-lift unless there was a guarantee of no reduction in the manning scales.

But this decision was ignored. On the following Monday, two fork-lifts were introduced. The manning scales? Instead of the custom and practice of employing seven quayside gangs of eight men, a total labour force of fifty-six, paid at the piecework rate of 3s. a ton of general cargo divided by eight, the seven gangs were reduced to two, with three men in each. That was fifty men no longer required, and to rub salt into the wound, the general cargo rate was HALVED. So the machine was not only being paid for by a reduction in the labour force, it was also halving the cargo rate from 3s. a ton to 1s. 6d. Progress indeed! How many times have you heard that crap about wages forcing up prices? As a result of the cut in the labour costs there should have been a corresponding cut in the port charges to the shippers —but not a farthing came off. Do you wonder that registered portworkers get up in arms at the mention of increased mechanisation and "modernisation"? A reduced labour force, instead of creating unemployment—sorry! I'm always forgetting to use the more respectable term *redundancy*—ought to result in a shorter working week with increased pay and fringe benefits resulting from the increased profits. But that would be asking too much in the name of progress!

Here's some more evidence to undermine all that con stuff about wages forcing up prices. During world war two, all meat was bought from the Commonwealth countries in bulk; it was far too dangerous for the meat-merchants' buyers to go out and buy according to grade and fix the profit margin accordingly, so the Government did the bulk buying and the meat merchants were given a subsidy. Funny! The meat tasted just the same; lamb was lamb and mutton was mutton and you didn't have to have it graded to decide which was which. For the dockers on piecework, this system was simpler and quicker. But within a year or two of the end of the war (and food rationing) the Government gave up bulk buying and the merchants resumed their former practice: meat was selected on the Commonwealth farms, selected, graded and priced according to its grading, and each merchant had his meat marked. This in turn meant that all meat discharged on the quayside had to be sorted according to the merchants' marks—after all, that's what each had bought and that's what he demanded. This meant that the momentum of the piecework was slowed down, effecting a major cut in piece-work earnings. After a few days of unrest and argument, including some withdrawal of labour, the employers, in agreement with the unions involved, conceded that extra men should be employed in the gangs for sorting of marks and grades and that an extra 5s. per four-hour shift and 2s. 6d. for a two-hour period of over-time should be paid *pro rata* to the peace work payment. For a few years there was peace on the meat front. Naturally the piece workers became more expert at sorting and the momentum built up; payment by results produced bigger average earnings—and of course bigger and better profits. But this was too much for the employer. It choked him to think of pay-packets getting bigger. Accordingly the employers made out the case to the trade union's rates committee that the sorting of meat was no longer an en-cumbrance on the piece-work momentum and produced wage bills to support their argument, calling for the ending of the meat-sorting allowance of 5s. a session.

Instead of the unions demanding to see the profits that the energy of the men had earned the employers (for after all the purpose of piece work was to create the incentive to do more— more profits for the employer, more wages for you) the unions agreed to end the sorting money. The employers softened the blow with an offer of a provisional 9d. for every hundred carcases discharged over the existing rate. This was accepted, after much resentment, by the meat men. But of course the meat workers, to compensate for the loss of the 12s. 6d. sorting money, began to drive themselves harder and harder to get the extra 9d. per hundred—you've got to go a long way to beat the shipowners and meat merchants at the cut-and-thrust, no doubt about it. Eventually the obvious happened. The employers began to moan at the wage-bills for piece work gangs and started nagging for the removal of the 9d. per hundred extra.

The trade union officials finally gave way, without demanding to see the profits that had been made as a result of the 9d. Had they done so, the employers would have shut up like clams. So there you are. Within a few years the meat men had lost 12s. 6d. a day sorting money plus a provisional 9d. per hundred extra. Which meant that on an average four-and-a-half working-day ship of approximately quarter of a million lambs, it was worked out by some of the export meat tally-clerks that the employer was saving in labour costs approximately £6 per man employed. Was there any corresponding cut in the price of meat in the butchers' shops? So wages are responsible for high prices? What happened between the years from one wage-increase to the next—did prices stand still? Back Britain! If we were to give a voluntary half-hour's overtime, do you think there would be a corresponding cut per pound in the price of meat? Who are they trying to con?

13

A Day on the Waterfront

Come with me, dear reader, sceptic or critic, on a visit to the Royal Group of docks, Sector 4, waterfront. Wait with me at 6.15 a.m. on a bitter cold January morning at the bus stop in Commercial Road, Stepney. Cool your anger if after blowing on your cold hands for fifteen minutes, you find the on-coming bus is full up; regulars are immune from rage after many hard winters. Board the next one, number 40A. Stand all the way for your one-and-fourpenny fare (just a few years ago it cost you 7d.). Jump off at the Queen Victoria Dock viaduct and gaze for a moment at the breaking dawn, a red ball of fire showing through the fast-moving night clouds, casting a glow of colour on the murky waters of the largest sheet of enclosed water in the world.

The quayside cranes tower skywards, silhouetted against the red-brick warehouses, awaiting "starter's orders" to discharge the merchandise from the ships' holds—flour, paper, timber, grain, meat and butter, chilled beef, bales of rubber, palm kernals, coffee, crates of fruit and tins of pineapple. Many artists, famous and unknown, have transferred this fascinating panorama to canvas. Look down, reader. You are gazing on a chess board where (to sneak a line from Omar Khayyam) "destiny with seven thousand pieces plays". There are more problems on this chess board than on those of the masters at the Hastings Chess Tournament. It's not a problem of white and black to move or draw; its a problem of worker and employer to move and win.

Leave the board and come with me to see the "pieces". The time is now 7.20 a.m. The place is the main gates of the Royal Group of docks—Albert and Victoria. Let's stand here on "speakers' corner" near the Connaught, a very old public-house of Georgian architecture—known all over London's waterfront ever since the days of sail. The traffic is beginning to build to a peak, long-distance lorries, private cars, all sorts of vehicles. And a crowd of men is gathering, old, middle-aged, young, some hatless, some wearing the good old cloth cap, all tough-looking, with the complexion of those who live an outdoor life. You will observe some of them breaking off their conversations to consult a glass case which displays a printed sheet indicating the names of the shipping companies requiring labour; it is known officially as the work sheet but colloquially as the slave sheet. This is where the opening gambit on the chess board begins.

If it were possible to take a look into their thoughts as they scrutinise the slave sheet I am quite sure some of them would read thus: here is a youngster looking at the meat firms' requirements because they have the best-paying piece-work rates; he is married, perhaps he has just moved, after living with his parents or his wife's parents, into a home of his own, so he needs more rent— landlords not being as kindhearted as dear old Mum and Dad— and he's saved enough with the help of his wife for the down payment on some furniture, but now she's pregnant and can't continue working so everything is up to him. He is weighing up his chances on that particular firm's call. Alongside him is an-other seeker; he's not feeling too good but he's got to get back to work, having just returned from weeks of sickness, exhausted all his Sick Club benefits and got into debt trying to provide food and clothing for a wife and three kids; he's not caring what sort of work it is as long as it's work. Here's another one; he's getting on in years and hopes to find a lighter job, working until 5 p.m.—he can't stand the cold for ten hours.

It's 7.35 now. Hundreds of men stream in through the gates, making their way to the various places for the general call-on, facing the firms' foremen and labour superintendents who will at exactly 7.45 a.m. walk over to the waiting labour-force and make their selection. The shorter men move in fast, trying to get a "fronter" so that they can be seen, for at times, particularly if there is a fall-off in shipping, the crowd on "the stones" can be four or five men deep and about 500 yards long.

Snatches of conversation can be heard: "Poxy Chelsea, let me down on the easy six—" "What do you think of Billy Elliot's gang, working through all that rain, they ought to be dog-knotted!" —"Did you hear about So-and-so getting done—?"

Across the road the foremen are synchronising their watches. Some of the men are practising hypnotism, staring at the back of the neck of a particular foreman in the hope that when he turns round they'll be the first one he'll catch sight of an call on. At another place of call, you'll perhaps hear the fly-boys remarking that such-and-such a firm has got a good job—hoping that some of the inexperienced youngsters will rush down to that place of call and leave this one clear for the fly-boys.

All of a sudden there is a complete hush. Everyone is standing still, expectant and anxious. The smaller men at the rear stand on tiptoe. Over walk the ship and quay foremen, like a Sheriff's posse in a Western. Charlie's gang! Smith's gang! Four men for *pro rata* on chilled beef! There is a rush and a flurry, arms are outstretched with registrations books in the hands (without the registration book you can't go to work). The little men in the front have been shoved aside. When there's been a heavy spell of unemployment, the call-on reminds you of a flock of seagulls converging on a morsel.

Those lucky enough to have been selected make their way to the job. Their next problem is: will it be 7 p.m. or 5 p.m.?—five o'clock's no bleedin' good—will it be under the crane or the winches?—invariably the power-crane is faster; it can be placed anywhere in the hold; but steam or electric winches call for extra effort.

Those who have not had the fortune to be called-on make their way to the centre control of Sector 4, and wait for the indent of labour from the shipping companies and the Port of London Authority, hoping against hope that they won't be allocated to a back-breaking turn or a "shit" job (colloquial for a badly-paid one).

When all the jobs are under way, the cut-and-thrust between the men and the employers begins. On arrival at the place of work aboard ship and quay, the ship's gangs remove the hatches of the hold, take a good look at the cargo and note how it has been stowed; they then make the necessary division of labour and commence work. After an hour or two, working with their expert knowledge and skill, based on years of experience, they sum up what the yield will be on a piece-work momentum in conjunction with the rate for the commodity they are handling. If the manner in which the cargo has been stowed creates obstacles to a piece-work output, they will stop the job, sum up what a day's output would yield over and above the time-rate, the agreed minimum hourly rate, and if the yield is too small to warrant an all-out

back-breaking piece-work effort, they will call in the ship's foreman and tell him that the job warrants extra men, plus money
to make it pay on a piece-work basis. The foreman informs the
labour superintendent, who will then come along, and a further
repetitive discussion takes place with the gang. The labour superintendent will make some tentative compromise; he can concede
the demand for extra men, but not for the money. The gang
must then telephone the local office for an area committee, consisting of representatives from the other firms operating within
the sector; these arrive at the appointed time, inspect the job to
their own satisfaction and then adjourn to the ship's cabin to
listen to the case set out by the trade union paid official, with
an observer from the gang in question. After having stated the
case and answered questions, the two latter retire while the area
committee deliberates. Meanwhile the gang continues to work a
time-rate speed and output. When the area committee has reached
a decision on the men's demands, the trade union official is
called in and informed. He returns to the gang and tells them of
the employers' reply and counter-offer, if any. The gang goes
into a huddle and confers, whether to accept or reject. The trade
union official takes their reply back, and if the gang has decided
to reject the employers' offer, the area committee deliberates
again.

If the ship is required to make her sailing date on time, to
avoid a stoppage or a refusal of piece work (in favour of a time-
rate that could delay the ship for many days) they will probably
agree to the first demand or step up their offer. Talk about cut-
and-thrust! It goes on all the time on London's waterfront.

If after all the employers are stubborn enough to stick to their
first decision and the gang refuses to compromise, the trade union
official has no alternative but to inform the men of their rights.
They can take the job on a time-work basis, or continue on a
piece-work stroke and have the matter referred to a special joint
meeting of employers and trade union in the City. If the men
won't accept either of these alternatives, they withdraw their
labour and place themselves on unofficial strike. Except on rare
occasions the recommended trade union alternatives are chosen—
in spite of the efforts of the national dailies to make you believe
that the irresponsible dock workers are prepared to strike on the
least pretext. No such thing. A decision to withdraw labour is
only taken after a deep, thoughtful appraisal of the situation. A

strike means going without wages. There are wives and families to think about. Only after exhausting all channels of negotiation, or if the provocation is too much to endure, will this step be reluctantly taken.

There's one big difference between this living game of chess and the game that is played on the conventional chess board; *the pawns are more powerful*—they can move and fight in all directions.

Let us finish this conducted tour of dockland with a couple of personal experiences. I had just finished a meat job. My part of the operation, with three others, was to raise the Argentinian chilled beef so as to enable the "backers" to step under and take it on their backs, run to the nearby meat haulage van and pitch tier on tier until the van was loaded. The weight of the beef, hind- or fore-quarter, would average about 120 lbs. The piece-work rate at so much per hundred averaged out at about 1½d per man per carcase.

On this particular day, prior to starting work, I had been speaking at the dock gate, urging the lads to attend their trade union branches and demand an upward revision of all piece-work rates. I quoted as an example the poor rate paid for carrying chilled meat. On my way to get my pay, I met one of the super-intendents—a friendly guy, but you can never tell how much is friendliness and how much is con: to be on the safe side, therefore, it's better to treat it as con. A few "vintage perms" (sorry, old hands) were standing around as we conversed, and he was trying a "Jack-the-lad" approach with his hail fellow well met stuff, but trying at the same time to undermine my remarks about the miserable rate for chilled beef. He built his case on the stupendous amount of some piece-work bills to the men, quite forgetting to mention their colossal output. "Of course, Jack old boy, your committee are completely irresponsible, just out to create unrest", was his line.

All those lads standing by were by now alert and interested, so I replied as customary with a simple analogy. "Excuse me, Mr Superintendent, may I put a case to you?" He agreed, and I continued. "Supposing you were to go home and find your wife out, and decided to cook your own meal. Perhaps you fancied a steak, but on looking in the fridge you found there wasn't any, so you decided to ask the neighbour's lad to go and get you some. . . ." The Superintendent is beginning to look superior and smug. ". . . When the kid got back from the butcher's, would you give him something?"

Everyone is now agog for Sir's reply. I think to myself, now you're going to be a real Jack-the-lad with your generosity. He is. "Oh, I'd certainly give the lad sixpence," he said. Immediately I replied: "So if you think a pound of steak is worth sixpence for carrying, how do you arrive at a payment of 1½d. to one of your men for running and pitching a piece of chilled beef weighing 120 pounds?" His Jack-the-lad attitude vanished in a flash as, amid laughter, he stormed off with a muttered remark about me being incorrigible.

It may not have been the same day, and probably wasn't, but I remember a typical November afternoon, cold and raining, as miserable as the economic situation. It was a Thursday, and a few ships had arrived, creating a demand for an allocation of men. Those of us who hadn't been employed since Monday could only earn their guarantee that week. I happened to be one of the unfortunates, but we had a laugh because one of the allocation men was very forthright and sarcastic when riled. The job we had been working on was of a heavy and arduous nature, and the character in question was in a very vinegary mood. We were approaching the main gate when the policeman on duty, known as Rosy Apples because of his country-boy complexion, came out of his box. With a disarming smile he challenged our friend Vinegar Joe in the customary phrase of the P.L.A. Police: "Excuse me, sir, do you happen to have anything in your possession that doesn't belong to you?"

Vinegar Joe was at his angriest best. "Yes, the horn," he replied.

"Now, sir, I don't want any of that," bridled Rosy Apples.

"Who's asking you! It's for my old woman," retorted Vinegar Joe, and strolled on, leaving the rest of us rolling with laughter and Rosy Apples standing there speechless.

Finally, to complete the day, as I leave the dock, checking my wage packet, I catch up with a bent-over figure trailing a slight limp—Vinegar Joe, muttering to himself as he too checks his pay. "What's the trouble, Joe?" I ask. "They given you too much?"

He gives me a scornful look. "Too much? Why, that dirty, thievin' whoreson at Thievin' Lane"—he was referring to the Local Tax Inspector, and Thievin' Lane was the dockers' term for Seething Lane where the Tax Inspector has his office—"he's nicked three quid off me. Once I get through the gate it'll be like goin' to the cleaners. I'll go to the Connaught and order a pint of ale, and that'll be taxed. A packet of 'snout' [cigarettes] and they'll be taxed. Take the bus and pay a shillin' for a fare that was once sixpence. Go to the hairdresser, used to call himself a barber, 'do you want it styled, sir?', mustn't give less than a tanner tip or he'll cut my bleedin' ear off next time. Walk indoors, give the old gooseberry her whack—and it's got to be a whack to pay a £4-a-week rent. Shilling each to the kids. And when all that's done, my share after fifty hours of piece-work is about fifty bob—and out of that I've got to put my fares aside. You call that too much?"

We couldn't help laughing, I and the chaps who were with me. I went home and told Ellen and she laughed too. But it's no joke really.

14

Disunity a Tragedy

I have taken an active part in every major post-war dock strike since 1945. Looking back, it seems to me that—with one exception—every one of them has been worth while; for apart from the (very few) that were connected solely with the wage packet, they have been actions to uphold the principles of trade unionism, international brotherhood, protection for our aged members, support for other trade groups of the transport industry—meat haulage drivers, fruit market workers, porters and drivers—and above all for the dignity of labour.

The one exception was the tragic inter-union struggle that reached a crisis in the year 1955 and broke into a strike between the two most important trade unions serving the port of London's Thames riverside, from the upper reaches of Brentford and Fulham down to Tilbury, the gateway to the estuary.

The struggle stemmed from the rival antagonisms between the executive committee of the National Amalgamated Stevedores' & Dockers' Union and the London and National docks' trade groups of the Transport & General Workers' Union, then under the leadership of General Secretary Arthur Deakin. Between the rank and file of the two unions, no such antagonisms existed; there was a warm comradeship between docker, stevedore and clerk, working side by side on ship and quay, sharing the same back-breaking toil, the same hardship and prosperity, full employment or under-employment according to the ups and downs of the trade situation—resulting from the failure of successive governments, Conservative or Labour, to plan a stable economy, and their cap-in-hand tie-up with the almighty dollar. The rank and file were too busy struggling for a decent living standard for their families to engage in rivalry with one another. They were of one accord.

H

The tragic inter-union struggle, however, arose from the long-standing dissatisfaction of the portworkers of Merseyside, Manchester and Hull with the service they received from the full-time officials of the Transport & General Workers' Union dock trade groups. These officials constantly rode roughshod over the appeals of their members, refusing to defend the demands of their rank and file and—so it was alleged—collaborating with the dock employers against them. Eventually, after repeated demands for an enquiry by the docks trade groups, several thousand men left the Transport & General Workers' Union and applied for membership of the National Amalgamated Stevedores' & Dockers'. After long and deep consideration, the executive of the N.A.S.D. decided to accept them, and in due course offices were set up on the northern ports.

Meanwhile, a strike broke out in the affected northern ports and later spread to London. It lasted five weeks and created a terrible bitterness not only between worker and worker but even within families. Brothers or cousins who happened to be on opposite sides, each loyal to the policy of his own union, would walk past one another like strangers. I knew of one father and son who would not eat at the same table.

In Sector 4 of the Royal Group and Sector 1 of the Surrey Dock, the N.A.S.D. had a strong, loyal, militant membership. We T.&G.W.U. men were torn between two loyalties; our own trade union executive had directed us to remain at work, but what were we to do when our fellow trade unionists, on strike, appealed to us not to cross the picket line? For myself, although I considered that the northern lads had justifiable grievances, I could not agree on the walkout, but at the same time I could not cross the picket line.

Eventually it was decided that the case should go before the Executive of the Trades Union Congress, the family of British trade unionism. The T.U.C. reached the verdict that the N.A.S.D. was in breach of the Bridlington Agreement, which stated that no affiiliated union of the T.U.C. should set up an office in an area or region where it had never had previous influence. The N.A.S.D., having done just that, was therefore instructed to return their membership cards to the breakaway members and advise them to return to their former union. The executive of the N.A.S.D., after hours of strong and bitter discussion, accepted the findings of the T.U.C. and made preparations to carry out its instructions. But this met with tremendous resentment from the rank and file, and an injuction was taken out to contest the decision of the N.A.S.D. executive in the High Court. The Court ruled against the decision, since the N.A.S.D. had no rule which enabled them to expel the White union men in accordance with Bridlington, and because they were outnumbered by the influx of White-card men from the northern ports they had no means of changing the rules. Costs were awarded against the N.A.S.D., amounting to approximately £5,000. This was a huge financial blow to such a small union. The money was raised by the loyal stevedores, dockers and clerks by means of a levy on contributions paid over a number of years.

The aftermath of this tragic inter-union schism was a bitter one. Wounds were caused that have taken years to heal—despite the continuous appeal of the Royal Group liaison committee, six men hammering away at early morning meetings at the dock gates with speeches and leaflets, to bury the hatchet and return to that unity that in the post-war period had been such a thorn in the side of the employers.

Slowly and gradually, the Royal Group liaison committee has become accepted by the rank and file of both unions, "Blue" and "White". Docker, stevedore and clerk have come to recognise us as men with a single purpose—to help forward the fight for decent conditions of employment, a proper basic wage, three weeks' holiday, a fall-back guarantee equal to the basic minimum, sick and accident benefits and the pensions due to those who have spent their strength and skill in the service of their fellow countrymen.

15

Self-sacrificing People

It was the summer of 1960, and four of us were travelling by train to Liverpool, to discuss with our Merseyside brothers the line of action to be taken in order to secure a worthwhile increase on the basic minimum. Oliver Williams and myself were members of the Royal Docks liaison committee, the other two—Freddie Francis and Harry Brown were very active militant members working in the short sea trade area, Tooley Street in what is known as the Pool of London.

Harry Brown, a fine lad, young and full of enthusiasm, married and with a family, was very popular in the Royal Group of Docks. Freddie Francis, also a family man, a loyal member of the Labour Party, had given tremendous service over the years in the trade union branch and higher committees of Sectors 2, 7 and 9 in the Pool of London; the men had a deep regard for his self-sacrificing efforts on their behalf. Oliver Williams, always referred to as Olly, was the father of four children; his wife, Rene, and he had lived through a long, hopeless and frustrating period before they were fortunate enough to obtain a house, and because of this both were exceptionally active in helping people who were homeless and living in centres. Rene was a tower of strength to Olly.

The conversation on the journey swung from boxing and football back to the docks. Olly began to talk about the lack of help from the trade unions when men suffered from long periods of sickness or injury, after exhausting all their private sick and accident benefits, and the plight of the widows of port registered workers. He thought something should be done about it. This caused Freddie and Harry to tell us about a scheme they were operating in their area. They were running a shilling-a-week football sweep, of which sixpence per member was paid into a distress fund and the rest went into prizes, with a top prize of £100. From the distress fund, £75 was paid to a widow or next of kin whether the deceased had died as the result of an industrial accident or through illness. Money grants were also made to members who had exhausted all their private sick benefits.

Olly sat silent and thoughtful as they talked, and afterwards plied them with questions. Our weekend on Merseyside was successful—we were warmly received by the Liverpool lads, whose friendship had gone on growing since the early post-war struggles. On the Monday morning, Olly told us that he'd been so deeply impressed by the work done by Freddie and Harry that he was going to tender his resignation from the liaison committee in order to launch a distress fund for the Royal Group of Docks. Our committee wished him success in his endeavours. Within a week he had enlisted the interest of some very militant lads, and the Royal Docks Distress Fund came into being on August 20, 1960.

There are not enough words in the English language to give full praise to the magnificent, self-sacrificing work done by the men who run this Fund. What tremendous courage they started with! Their first difficulty was to get the men to join. They had to overcome the poisonous whispering of certain London docks officers of high standing who tried to sow the seeds of distrust— obviously because they were known militants. But the greatest obstacle arose with in the first week of their inauguration. Three members died, and here they were, a committee without any funds, pledged to pay benefits of £75 to three widows. All eyes were upon them—those of the reluctant, the sceptics and the ill-wishers in particular. But these lads, true to their splendid principles, borrowed the money and paid out £75 to each of the unhappy widows. From then on there was a rush for membership. The critics and doubters were silenced, and the poison-tongues could no longer spit out their venom.

How about this for outstanding achievement in self-sacrificing endeavour? Since its commencement on August 20, 1960, the Fund had paid out £28,275 in death benefits, £21,765 in sick benefit, £21,500 in distress benefits, £11,200 to retired members and £72,800 in prize money.* They have organised social events, dances, river boat shuffles to France, boxing tournaments and family sports days. It is interesting to note that the first river boat

---

* This was up to the time of writing, Summer 1968.

shuffle was held to celebrate the seventy-fifth anniversary of the famous dock strike of 1889 (the strike for the Dockers' Tanner); the national and London official dock trade groups failed to celebrate this officially and have offered no help to the Distress Fund. Every penny collected and paid out has been raised by a small group of dedicated men—not one paid official among them. Day in day out, early morning before commencement of work, in their dinner hour, you will see them going around, membership book in one hand and pencil in the other, often giving credit out of their own pockets to those they haven't managed to contact, or members out on sick or accident, in order that their membership should not lapse and disqualify them from benefit.

Every service, which also entails their weekends, is given freely. If we had an industrial Honours List, their names should go at the top: Olly Williams, Don Perry, Ted Kirby, George Smith, Bill Lee, Bill Knight, Tom Ross, Jimmy Grey, M. Bentham, Ernie Rice, George Springford, Joe Quinn, George Fry, George Huzzy, Tim Driscoll—sixteen selfless men whose matchless work has put an end to a century of indignity whereby the lame and the sick stood with cap in hand begging for alms, ignored by the trade union establishment of the Port of London. This is the sort of service that deserves knighthoods: real and sincere service for their fellow men.

On Christmas Eve that same year, 1960, I was walking past the control point office of Sector 4 on my way home. It was 1 o'clock and I had been excused by the employers for the afternoon, like thousands of other dock workers fortunate enough to have been at work under the continuity rule. I became aware of the noise of angry voices, and looking down into the control pen I could see hundreds of men hollering and shouting, with angry gesticulations, banging on the control windows almost to the point of smashing them. I went down to enquire what it was all about, and was told that the Control Manager was insisting that the men who had failed to obtain work in the morning must put their books in and be directed to work as requested by the Port of London Authority, to fill the vacant positions created by their own weekly workers failing to turn up for the afternoon period. Naturally the Pool lads resented this demand. They considered, and rightly, that they were being used as make-shift, and they wanted equality with those who had been at work in the morning. Besides they wanted to go home and help their wives and mothers to do the Christmas Eve shopping. But the Sector Manager, a zealot for the rules of the National Dock Labour Board, had said that unless his instruction was carried out they would lose their entitlement to the Christmas holiday payment.

Having gathered what it was about, I approached the Sector Manager with a request that he should get in line with the spirit of Christmas, goodwill to all men, and relax the rule for once in the year. No, he insisted on it being carried out to the letter.

When the lads were informed of this the situation reached riot pitch. But with the assistance of Roy Tierney, who happened to be one of the men affected, calm was restored, and we advised every man to put his work-book in—but then to walk away and refuse any allocation for work. We then informed the Control Point Manager that if we found on resuming work after the holiday that the men were going to be disqualified from their holiday payments, we would convene a mass meeting and recommend a walk-out. A great cheer went up. Every man's book went sailing through the sector windows, and they all walked away to a man, calling out festive greetings to one another —and to Roy and me. Roy and I breathed sighs of relief and took leave of each other.

Christmas was over. It was December 29th. No decision had yet been reached concerning the holiday payment and I was sincerely hoping that commonsense would prevail. I had picked up a job with the Glen Line shipping company; working in a ship's gang, my part was to be on the quayside and make up the sets of cargo brought out to the ship's side by the quayside export gang, to be lifted and lowered into the hold for export. When the call for the tea-break was announced, my partner and I went aboard ship to take our tea at the hold we were working at. The rest of that day is a complete blank, a black-out, gone out of my life for good . . .

. . . My eyes flutter and I become aware of somebody bending over me . . . gradually I bring the apparition into focus. . . . I see a very dark-skinned face, with a big, warm smile, and hear a soft contralto voice asking: "How do you feel? Lie still, and I'll bring you a drink of milk!" I must be dreaming . . . I snuggle down to catch some more sleep before the alarm clock goes off.

Again I am aware of wakening. This time I can see my wife, Ellen. Looking sad and anxious, she is repeating the words of the dark-skinned apparition: "How do you feel?" She bends over and kisses me and says I must try not to cough, as the doctors are worried about pneumonia setting in. . . . I must still be dreaming! But from then onwards, I see a succession of well-known faces—my daughter Kathleen and her husband, Olly Williams, Roy Tierney, Johnnie Madget. I begin to realise that it is no dream. Something has happened to me and I am in hospital.

The next time I see Ellen I am able to talk, and she tells me that on the previous day I had fallen down the ship's hold from top to bottom—a distance of about 53 feet. While we are talking, the day nurse comes to take my temperature; here is my apparition, but now I know she's real, and comes from Nigeria. We have a lot of conversation later on.

Roy Tierney and Olly Williams come again to visit me. I ask them what has happened about the threat of the London Board to withhold the holdiay payment, and they tell me not to worry, the Board has decided to take no action. That's good news and now I can relax and concentrate on getting better.

I had got off lightly. Apart from concussion, I sustained a broken clavicle and collar bone, three broken ribs and some deep contusions. When I thought of my old friend and comrade the late Wally Jones, I realised what a narrow escape I had had. Roy jokingly reminded me that Lenin had said: "Not yet, there is too much to be done."

I've been a vegetarian for many years and have always tried to keep fit, and Nature was very kind to me. Within a week I became a walking patient and was discharged to the outpatients' department. I decided to continue what treatment I needed at my own hospital, the Manor House at Golders Green, so ably administered by Mr A. Lane. I never cease to be amazed at the way this hospital provides such wonderful treatment for its members, for the low subscription of 6d. a week; I'd like to pay particular tribute to the blind therapist, Mrs MacDowell (lovingly referred to by everyone as Mrs Mac) who has nursed me with healing hands on every occasion I have attended for treatment. I am sure my feelings are shared by thousands of workers in all parts of the country who have been Manor House patients. Yet for some unknown reason there are still many trade union branches whose members do not subscribe. I urge them to join. Manor House membership may be the key to their health as it has been to mine.

Under the skill of the doctors and the physiotherapy department, I mended quite speedily and resumed work fit and well within three months. But (after a two years' wait) I lost my legal action against the employers for liability. I applied for legal aid from the National Insurance and Social Security, having to fork out £78 myself towards the cost of the action. Two witnesses who were working in the ship's hold at the time of the accident appeared on my behalf. The presiding judge decided to accept the statement of the ship's foreman who contradicted my claim of neglect on the part of the shipping company. Costs were awarded against me, but the company refrained from claiming.

16

United Strength

I count 1962 as a historic year. For the first time in the post-war
period, the accredited dock trade unions won a wage increase
from the port employers by threatening to use the united strength
of 63,000 registered port workers to end all the national agreements and withdraw their labour. The employers, right from the
start of the negotiations, had refused to concede a wage increase
above the 3 per cent level laid down was a wage policy by the
Tory government, and it was *their* government. However, they
were not prepared for the determined, strong and unarguable
case put forward on our behalf by Frank Cousins, General
Secretary of the Transport & General Workers' Union. Just
before midnight on Sunday, May 13th, faced with an official
national strike on the Monday morning, the 14th, and the risk
of increasing support that would have come from the rest of the
organised labour movement, the employers gave way and the
strike was called off.

What was important about this victory? One, it was a departure from the method of wage-negotiation that had been used in
the early post-war years—the cap-in-hand attitude. It was
negotiation from strength. Not only were the employers defeated;
the government's wage policy suffered a setback, and this gave a
lead to all the trade unions of the major industries to argue and
negotiate above the 3 per cent norm. It put new life into the
rank and file, giving them a renewed confidence in trade unionism and showing that where there is unanimity between the
leadership and the members on matters of policy, no employers
or government can withstand them.

Secondly, an attack was being prepared against the unions.
Twice the employers flatly rejected our claim, but when notice
was given that a national strike was being considered, they made

an offer. It was unsatisfactory to the unions and to the men. Pressure began to build up. Cabinet meetings were held to prepare for the use of troops in the docks. The dockers were told —as the railwaymen had been told—that you can't take the government on. But the rank and file, as represented at the national delegate conference, rejected a proposal for a week's postponement and made it quite clear that unless there was a better offer, both the bosses and the government would be faced with a national dock stoppage on Monday, May 14th. A better offer was made, and as a result of arguing from strength the trade unions gained most of their demands. Contrast this with the handling of the Engineers' claim; all Mr Carron's influence was used against industrial action or even the threat of it, and as a result the engineering and shipbuilding employers made no offer.

Thirdly, it proved that in the last resort industrial action is the only real weapon the workers have. Shadow-boxing is for the gym. Any line of argument used to justify inaction only benefits the employers. The screaming indignation in the headlines of the national Tory press was enough in itself to encourage all other workers to urge their claims with vigour.

In the same merry month of May 1962, I was deputed by the Liaison Committee of the Royal Group of docks to address the men and call for a one-hour stoppage in sympathy with the nurses, whose claim for an increase in the pittance they were paid had been turned down by the Tory Minister of Health, Enoch Powell. At that morning's mass meeting I dealt with the statement of Enoch Powell concerning the nurses' claim and reminded my hearers of the straits our industry would be in without them; not an hour, not a day goes past without some port worker needing their care and attention. I then called for the lads to vote with their feet in support of the nurses, by walking out of the dock at 11 a.m. in a one-hour token strike, to establish our anger and resentment at the insulting offer of a $2\frac{1}{2}$ per cent increase by the Minister of Health. The vote was unanimous. At exactly 11 a.m. the whole force of the Royal Group walked out, solid to a man.

The press took very little notice of this action. What a contrast to the hullabaloo they set up years later when a small minority of dockworkers walked out in a blaze of publicity for Enoch Powell's racist policies!

In 1963, Ellen and I became grandparents for the first time. Our daughter Kathleen had a baby girl, born (by Caesarian) at Reading General Hospital—the only non-Cockney in the family. Kathleen had told us that she intends to have a family of four and wants them while she is young. She feels it is wrong to have an "only child" (like herself); that a family of several children creates a better understanding of human relationships and responsibility to the community. Ellen and I are in complete agreement with her, and hope that the upbringing we have given Kathleen has helped to foster this unselfish attitude.

What an impact a first born child can have on a family! As the young parents gaze together at the result of their creative union, it seems to remove individual subjectiveness and replace it with a united parental objectiveness for the child's future. Both the young people seem to take on a new maturity. The grandparents feel elated—the grandmother in particular; it restores to her some of her former youth in a way more real and lasting than the most expensive beauty salon could do it (I mean you, Ellen!), because apart from the physical change there is that inner feeling of sharing, of being part of the new being that has come into the world.

As a result of slum clearance and road widening under the Greater London Plan, we moved in 1964 to a sixteen-storey skyscraper, and I chose a flat on the sixteenth floor which has a panoramic view of east London and the Thames. If it were customary to give names to flats as people do to private houses, I would call ours "The Eagle's Eyrie", though instead of looking down with penetrating eye on fields and meadows as the eagle does, I see a panorama of dockside boroughs on either bank of the river, eastward past Limehouse reach and the off shores of Surrey and Kent, with Greenwich Naval College and Observatory in the distance. Looking west, you can see Tower Bridge and the Tower of London, and beyond that the architectural splendour of Christopher Wren's St Paul's. Wherever you focus your eyes you recognise some historical landmark of our great metropolis.

As I look down into the neighbouring boroughs of Poplar and Stepney, those twin pioneers of struggle with their magnificent contribution to the proud industrial history of London trade unionism, co-operation and social reform, I get a feeling of confidence; confidence that, with correct, militant progressive

leadership my fellow-citizens will be second to none in the fight
to establish a real socialist Britain. At the risk of being called a
parochial chauvinist (can there be such a thing?) I get the feeling
as I look down that I am gazing at the pulse of life, that every
man, woman and child is related to, and part of, twentieth
century society and its culture: transport workers, seamen, train
and bus drivers, port workers, postal workers, medical and
social service workers, city clerks and stenographers, dustmen,
road-sweepers, schoolteachers and office cleaners—and not to be
part of them would be to resemble an amputated limb, of no
further use. Nothing amazes me more, as I travel around Britain
speaking in universities and other centres of culture, than the
students (usually non-grant students) who come up to me after
the meeting is over and begin: "You see, Mr Dash, I'm from the
middle-class really . . ." I tell them politely that that's a lot of
crap; that there are only two classes in society—those who own
the means of production and those who produce. Of course there
are different income groups, but to persist in being "middle-
class" is a confession of failure; there's the working class and
there's the upper class and here they are, high and dry, hanging
in the middle. It's the upper class that has made the idea of
working for a living undignified when it should be the reverse;
it's the working people, including the salaried and professional
groups, who should walk with dignity. We are the creative class;
it's those who take the lion's share in our productive effort and
create nothing themselves who should feel undignified.

I even know working people who tend to make excuses for
being members of the working class, who speak of themselves as
"only a worker" and think that culture has nothing to do with
them. Why, everything that is man-made is the result of the
creative class; all culture, and even the language, developed from
work, from the way that societies obtained their livelihood.
Being a member of the working class gave me the confidence that
I could write this autobiography without seeking the aid of a
ghost writer; it's perhaps not as grammatically pure as one could
wish, but I am articulate and if the reader is not familiar
with some of the colloquialisms, anyway it is in English, our
mother tongue.

We like our flat. It is very functional, with every room capturing
light and as we sit at our meals in the kitchen Ellen and I can see
tramp steamers and tugs sailing to and fro along the Thames.

But even those fortunate enough to have homes must fight for them: any worker knows that an increase in rent can be regarded as a wage cut, a threat to our living standards. Since the election of the Conservative Greater London Council, all council tenants are threatened with a cut in their living standards because of the intention to increase rents on the housing estates by 70 per cent. Since the announcement of this intention, tenants' associations have sprung into being almost overnight on every estate. A young fellow-tenant and I decided to form one for our estate. We set about drawing up a leaflet, distributed it to every family in the flats, and convened a meeting at which a Tenants' Association came into being with myself elected as Chairman.

No action to date has been taken by the Prices and Incomes Board against the rises in rents. In fact, a member of the Labour Cabinet, M.P. for an historical Labour borough, when approached by some of his constituents in a lobby, replied with the fighting statement: "It will have to be phased." No anger. No protest. With his salary of approximately £9,000 a year, he tells his constituents he would recommend "phasing"—like a parent telling a child that he's got to swallow a bottle of castor oil: "I know it's nasty, but I'll give it to you a spoonful at a time", (but you'll get the bottleful just the same). He showed no concern for the hardship that will be experienced by the tenants. You can cut down on pleasure, or even on food if that is necessary, but you can't cut down on rent. Every Monday morning the collector is at the door; the local-government landlord won't accept any hard-luck story, and there's no chance these days of "doing a moonlight flit" as our parents and grandparents did in the old days with the slum landlord. There has got to be resistance against rent increases—along with the battle in industry against the Prices and Incomes Policy (or even the voluntary wage-vetting system proposed by the T.U.C.). We're constantly told that "we" are spending too much, while out of the other corner of its mouth the government insists that we spend 70 per cent more on rent. It doesn't make sense.

17

The Charter

The continuation of casual employment in one of Britain's major industries is a scandal. There is no security of employment from day to day. Worker is compelled to compete against worker for a job. The labour force was divided into "pool" and "perm", the pool men contracted out to shipping firms and stevedoring contractors, the perm men serving as weekly workers for a single employer. The iniquity of two calls a day for the hiring of men, in order to keep them at the employers' beck and call, forces wasted days on the men and is open to abuse and corruption.

In 1963, the employers put forward a "de-casualisation plan" the purpose of which, as far as we could see, was to negate the power of the National Dock Labour Board, jointly controlled by the employers and the trade unions under the government's Dock Labour Scheme of 1947. The Dock Labour Scheme was viewed by us as a first step on the road to de-casualisation, with a register of dock workers and a fall-back wage. But it was only a first step.

The major threat of the employers' scheme for de-casualisation was the proposal to cut manning scales (i.e., to reduce the gang strengths) to do away with the Continuity Rule—the most cherished of all our protective practices, as I explained earlier, which they have been consistently warned to leave alone; to introduce so-called mobility of labour, make cuts in overtime payments, and reintroduce weekend working. It envisaged no more than 80 per cent de-casualisation anyway.

The 1963 plan was defeated by the refusal of the trade unions concerned to have anything to do with it. But the employers never give up. And in 1965, when we got the first hint that the government and the employers were going to have another try, a sort of preliminary whiff of Devlin, the London Liaison Committee began to think what should be done.

Our evenings, Saturday mornings and dinner-hours were spent in drafting an eleven-point programme which we called "The New Dockers' Charter". When this had been hammered out, we convened a mass meeting at the Town Hall in Canning Town, to put it before our fellow workers. After much keen questioning and discussion, the Charter was unanimously adopted. The Liaison Committee then set about having it printed in thousands of copies for distribution in London and all other parts. Copies were sent to the leading officials of the trade unions serving the industry, to the Prime Minister and to the Minister of Labour.

These were the terms of the Charter:

Phase 1
1. The National Dock Labour Board to maintain full control, i.e. contractors of labour, discipline, social welfare.
   Present strength of register to remain, no cutting in the manning scales, weekly worker register to be frozen, no make up of wastage.
2. All unregistered port workers to be governed by the scheme.
3. Fall-back pay to be £18 10s. 0d., each day to remain on its own—no devaluation, no disentitlement on failure to prove.
4. Forty-hour, five-day week. One call a day. No shift work.
5. Overtime payment to be excluded from fall-back guarantee.
6. Upward revision of piecework rates.
7. Sickness and accident pay to be 50 per cent of National average wage.
8. Retiring pensions to be 50 per cent of National average wage, exclusive of National Insurance payments. Retiring age at National Insurance level.
9. Three weeks' holiday at national average pay. Free or reduced transport fares on all shipping.
10. Trade unions to enforce no–soliciting rule.

Phase 2
11. Nationalisation of the industry.

With a record of increased production year after year (providing it had been a year of full employment) and with record profits to correspond—and an increasing accident rate—we were confident that had the Charter been adopted it would have put an end to our century-old ways of working, and would change the industry into an efficient modern service, benefiting the national economy and giving good wages coupled with the highest standards in social benefits and amenities, so vitally necessary for the dignity of labour. This could only be achieved by the removal of the national dock employers, who had milked our industry of £178,000,000 since 1948 and had scarcely put a penny back into capital investment to modernise the ports.

In support of our criticisms, I quote from a series of articles printed in *The Times* of January 4–8, 1965: "A nineteenth-century system, ill suited to modern needs . . . there is so much wrong about it . . . the traditional picture is a series of individual interests along the chain, each concerned with extracting what profit he can by providing what service he can to his own immediate customers . . . though the movement of goods from one customer to another ought to be a continuous, integrated process, it has never been anyone's job to see that it was . . . the country abounds with ports with surplus capacity of the wrong kind or in the wrong place." No wonder the series was entitled *Chaos in the Ports*!

The key, we maintained, lay in Point 10 of our Charter—nationalisation of the industry in a socialist manner, with workers' control. We were emphatic that any attempt to interfere with the National Dock Labour Board would meet with resistance.

At this particular period, militancy on the waterfront was at a low ebb. But our liaison committee, from past experience, was well aware that whilst workers are sleeping, the corridors of power are full of scheming. We decided to scheme likewise. An all-out campaign was launched, with continuous agitation, dock-gate meetings of explanation—particularly for the younger members—leaflets, and visits to other ports to address meetings. Bristol was the first port we approached. We went down by car to a convened meeting on a Saturday morning. It was well-attended, and I had the pleasure of addressing for the first time the men of Bristol, who had a good militant past, particularly during the Canadian Seamen's strike. The meeting resulted in the formation of the Bristol liaison committee, under the chairmanship of Brother McGrath, a capable orator and trusted spokesman.

Our next port of call was Southampton. There the set-up was

I

different. I met a convened meeting consisting only of militant trade union lay officials. Strangely, although the Southampton men have a militant record concerning local port problems, they are somewhat sectarian in their relationship with London and other ports. They have great confidence in two very capable men, Jack Bonner and Trevor Stallard. Their problems were easier to approach because all the workers in the port were members of a single branch of the Transport and General Workers' Union, and they did not feel there was any need to set up a liaison committee. Nevertheless, they were in agreement with our eleven-point programme, with certain modifications.

Intense discussion took place in every port of the country around the need for change, the statements of the employers, the proposals of the National Joint Council of the industry and the Rochdale Report (Lord Rochdale and his Committee had been asked: "To consider to what extent the major Docks and Harbours of Britain are adequate to meet present and future national needs; whether methods of working can be improved; and to make recommendations.") Following the Rochdale Report, fresh proposals from the employers appeared. They were akin to old wine in new bottles. In the Port of London, the proposal was for 100 per cent weekly engagement by firms operating in the enclosed docks, which cover only about 60 per cent of the men. The price for this would be a guaranteed weekly wage of £11 0s. 0d. complete mobility of labour, reduced gang strengths, night shift working, harsher discipline and a major attack on the right to strike, from which I quote: "*Any man taking part in a strike will forfeit all his rights to further benefit under his contract for so long as he withholds his labour. His contract may be cancelled depending on the circumstances of each incident*"—a clause tantamount to asking the trade unions to sign a victimisation agreement!

For other ports the same approach was shown, without even the same degree of weekly engagement being offered.

The Rochdale Committee endorsed this general approach, stating: "The general principles laid down as a basis for de-casualisation by the National Joint Council for the port industry are sound" (page 261, paragraph 652). Sound for whom? Not for the men. All that the proposals would mean for them was that in return for an extension of weekly engagement by the employers, they would have to agree to speed-up and increased exploitation, the fulfilment of the dream the port employers have cherished since 1945, highly mechanised ports working around the clock (it breaks their hearts to think of cranes standing still all night and losing two extra shifts which would mean clear profit—the first shift would take care of all the overheads), with a smaller labour force and a pool of casual labour to draw on in an emergency. What patriots they are!

I have said that the Dock Labour Scheme of 1947 was only the first step on the road to de-casualisation. But the employers had been whittling away even at this, by their increasing intro-duction of "perms" (now 22 per cent of the national register), by their frequent attempts to introduce compulsory overtime working, by their refusal to allocate work to all men in rotation, and by stepping up their use of non-scheme ports.* Progress to real de-casualisation can only be achieved on the basis of a single employing authority—and that can only be achieved by the socialist nationalisation of the port industry—Point 11 of the liaison committee's Charter. We are aware that this is a matter for Parliament, for political struggle. But we consider that the other ten points are a basis for ending the divisions within the industry and forming a united movement, for making the port industry efficient, progressive, economical in the service of the nation as a whole. The Charter has been drawn up and endorsed by those who do the work, whose skills, handed down from father to son, have made Britain's port industry the fastest and cheapest in Europe, second to only two Asian ports, Tokyo and Hong Kong (according to Sir Andrew Creighton, a former chairman of the port employers).

Had the Dockers' Charter been adopted, while awaiting the political decision on nationalisation, the bitter nine weeks' struggle arising out of the Devlin scheme would have been avoided. But no, it would be asking too much of the executives and the National Dock Labour Committee to swallow their pride and dignity and accept a plan from the servants' quarters: they preferred to go cap in hand to the employers, and came away discussing the employers' scheme.

Why the Devlin Scheme? How did it come about?

---

* Eleven ports that do not come within the Government's Dock Labour Scheme for registered port-employers under the National Dock Labour Board. They are in fact a rival power to the registered port employers: in times of industrial unrest, shipping is diverted to them. They will not even be brought in, I understand, with the proposed nationalisation of the port industry.

Before anyone in the trade union corridors of power or the executive suites of the shipping employers starts preening his plumage about what is good in the de-casualisation scheme, let me remind them that it was not of their making; it was the result of the campaign initiated by the unofficial Liaison Committee concerning a wage claim being negotiated by the accredited trade unions for the port industry. We on the Liaison Committee had learned that the terms of the wage negotiation spoke of "a substantial amount". Now, in our opinion, such terms of reference are ridiculous. Who is to determine what is meant by "substantial"? The employers? Why, an employer could claim that a halfpenny was a reasonable sum. It is this method of negotiation, rather than putting forward a straight demand for a named sum, that has been the reason for the port industry's basic wage being one of the lowest among the major industries—£9 9s. 2d. a week.

At all events, I was directed by the Liaison Committee to set in motion a campaign for the wage increase of not less than 25s. a week, with a corresponding percentage for the piece-worker. In the opinion of our committee, a wage increase must take some measurable step to meet three of the most important items which worry the wage or salaried worker—rent, rates and transport fares, and all of these were going up nearly as fast as the lifts in the GLC's skyscraper blocks. An increase of 25s. a week would be a step in the right direction, and I was directed to address the rank and file on the necessity of arguing for the 25s. as against "a substantial amount"—urging them to attend their local branches and demand this sum as the basis of negotiation.

The committee visited and corresponded with the other ports; funds were raised to print leaflets outlining our case; sticky-backs with the slogan "For 25s." were stuck all round London's waterfront; indoor meetings were convened. There was lobbying of dockland's Members of Parliament; gangs elected one of their number to go to Transport House or the employers' Federation House on the days when our negotiators met the employers; an hour's token stoppage was called for. Gradually the campaign grew in strength, causing alarm among the negotiators. Based upon my experience of the National Unemployed Workers' Movement of the 1930's (which showed the value of bringing your demands to the attention of the public) we had two enormous post-cards made. They were addressed to Sir Andrew

Creighton, chairman of the negotiating joint committee, and on the reverse side we stated our claim for the 25s. Now, our Post Office is one of the world's finest services—so long as you pay. These post cards were far too big to go through the letter-box, so the committee took them by van to the Post Office nearest to Federation House in Lower Thames Street, and paid the postage on them. From there they had to be carried by uniformed telegraph-boys, and were seen by thousands of City commuters on their way to work at 9.30 in the morning. They were delivered to Sir Andrew Creighton, who received them, no doubt, with good humour, but with an awareness that we of the rank and file meant business and were determined men.

The employers began to increase their offer, and the official trade union side changed their terms of reference from "a substantial amount" to 5s. a day—not 25s. a week; that would have meant identifying themselves too closely with the militants.

The campaign took on new strength. The lads in Liverpool, Hull and Bristol were pressing their demands on stronger lines. This began to have an effect on the employers, who, on July 7, 1964, considered the increase demanded by the work-people's side, which would raise the weekly time-rate from £9 9s. 2d. to £10 14s. 2d. and the piece-rate to 13.2 per cent. Negotiations on this claim proceeded and eventually, on August 28th, the following offer was made: that "subject to the agreement on the proposal for an examination of the position of the lower-paid workers, together with the review of the wage-structure of the docks industry and further talks in regard to the de-casualisation of the industry" they would increase the rates of pay to piece-workers by $3\frac{1}{2}$ per cent and the rate of time-workers by 2s. 6d. per day.

This offer was rejected by our negotiators, and we continued our campaign for the 25s. On October 1, 1964 the work-people's side suggested that a new approach should be made, involving a reappraisal of the whole structure of the industry from the angle of wages and from that of conditions of employment; meanwhile an interim payment should be made until a calm and intelligent assessment of the situation was possible. At the conclusion of the discussion, a proposal was drawn up on the following terms: that the employers' offer (2s. 6d. per day on the basic time rate and $3\frac{1}{2}$ per cent on the piece work rates) should be effective from October 5, 1964, adjustment of the fall-back payment of £9 0s. 0d.

to be recommended for acceptance by a docks delegate conference. It was also proposed that, subject to acceptance by the National Delegate Conference, a joint committee should be set up immediately to review the basic structure of the industry with particular reference to (1) Basic rates of pay; (2) Piece work and overtime payments; (3) Hours of work; (4) Holidays with pay; (5) Sick pay; (6) Fall-back pay and attendance money; (7) Social services and facilities in the docks; (8) Improved working arrangements. As several of the above questions are closely linked with the whole question of de-casualisation of the industry, it was further agreed that this vital problem should be re-considered.

There was a great deal of discussion over the word "interim" and the employers refused to accept it because they thought that it might be "misinterpreted".

The National Delegate Conference was fixed for October 7th and as soon as the liaison committee learned that the date was to be, we convened a mass meeting and called for a one-day token strike to take place on that date. This was unanimously accepted.

On the day of the National Delegate Conference, a rally, with posters, was held at Westminster under the shadow of Big Ben— who incidentally had both his hands up in approval, because he was chiming the hour of ten o'clock. We formed up by threes and, in torrential rain, with police escorting us, made ready to march to Transport House, Smith Square, to demonstrate our firm demand for an increase of 25s. and at the same time to welcome the national delegates as they arrived from other parts of the country. Soaked to the skin, a good thousand London portworkers—dockers, stevedores, clerks, old, middle-aged and young—surrounded the entrance to Transport House, proud and defiant, shouting with one united voice:

> "One, two, three, four, five,
> Nothing less than twenty-five!"

and watched the delegates arrive, with many pats on the back and much shaking of hands for those whom we knew personally, especially those from Liverpool and Hull with whom we have forged such close affinity in the struggles of the post-war years.

When the last man had entered Transport House, the London lads retired to a nearby pub to refresh themselves. We members of the liaison committee kept to our rule—never to meet (as a committee) in pubs—and settled down in the nearest cafe for tea or coffee and a discussion of the previous week's happenings and the prospects of the conference. After about an hour, we decided to go back to Transport House and give our ears a chance. As we neared the pub we could hear the strains of "Kevin Barry" and "John Brown's Body". The lads were warming up, and there was an anxious look on the faces of the coppers outside. Then someone came out of the pub and asked me to go and have a talk with the proprietor. The rest of the liaison committee came into the saloon bar with me. From all sides we were greeted with shouts of "Good old Jackie!" "Good old Vic!" "Watcher, Wal?" "How's it going, Davie boy?' We found the proprietor, his face as white as his luncheon table-cloths. "What's the trouble?" I asked him.

"Well, Mr Dash, all my ham, chicken and beef has disappeared. It's almost lunch time, and I haven't got a thing left!"

"That's all right," said Vic. "You want to sell out, surely?"

"Yes," said the proprietor, "but I've received no cash at all, and what about my regulars?"

We told him not to worry, to leave it to us. With that I stood on a chair and announced: "I know it's all been well-cooked and tasty, but don't let us down! How about a whip-round?"

"Stop worrying, Jack, it will be taken care of," was the reply. Within half an hour it had all been settled; the anxious look was removed from the proprietor's face, and all the lads were outside Transport House waiting for the delegates to emerge.

Suddenly there was a hush, as a group of men came down the steps. "What's happened?" we shouted.

Jackie Lydon, a very militant delegate from Merseyside, told us. "We turned down the recommendation from Frank Cousins and O'Leary for the acceptance of 12s. 6d."

There was a big roar of approval, coupled with growls of anger and dismay at the failure of the National Joint Council (of the accredited trade unions) to press for the 25s. Nevertheless, we members of the Liaison Committee were assured that our campaign over the previous months had made an impact on the national ports, and we were confident for the future.

The National Joint Council and the employers now faced an impasse. It was agreed to set up a committee of enquiry, responsible to the Minister of Labour. Its chairman was Lord Devlin, a retired High Court Judge, a very capable and learned Judge in his own profession; the Establishment think highly of him because he has sat on many public enquiries in previous troubles in the docks (though he never found the formula).

But why it was found necessary to call in high-ranking judiciary officials of the legal system to straighten out the docks industry and make it efficient puzzles me. Who knows more about the industry than the docks trade unions and the rank and file— the mechanics of the industry, with a century of skills behind them, handed down from father to son—who have produced fabulous profits for those avaricious shipowners, stevedoring companies and wharfingers? These men, if given a chance with the nationalisation of the ports, under workers' control, could turn it into an efficient, profitable and progressive industry, capable of serving the nation and the people out of all comparison to its past. I am confident that if there were anything wrong with Ray Gunter's or Lord Devlin's cars, they wouldn't go asking the milkman to put it right; no, they'd go to the mechanics of the industry, the men who have the know-how. And when the enquiry is set up, who is it that the committee sends for to tell them about the industry and what is considered necessary to make it efficient? (I myself was invited by Lord Devlin to attend Phase 2 of the Enquiry and submit my opinions and answer questions; very courteously received and listened to I was, and I am pleased to state that among the observations I made, the one about shop stewards became part of the recommended proposals.)

The committee's decision on Phase 1 of the enquiry was:

"Since the daily rate plays an important part in the wage structure of the industry, it is necessary to have a weekly rate divisible by five. Accordingly, we take the figures of 19s. 2d. weekly and 3s. 10d. daily as the rate increase we recommend."

I want to give a further quote from the report on Phase 1, because it gives the lie to the odious gutter-statements that have appeared in the national press (and still do) creating in the minds of the readers the impression that the dockers are a lazy, indolent lot with no sense of responsibility.

"In 1948 the average docker was responsible for the move-ment of 732 tons of cargo, while in 1963 he was responsible

Morning Star   THE AUTHOR WITH MERSEYSIDE LIAISON DELEGATES

WITH FRANK COUSINS AT THE ROYAL ALBERT DOCK GATE   *Morning Star*

Daily Sketch   A LECTURE AT CAMBRIDGE UNIVERSITY

THE AUTHOR AS ARTIST WITH ONE OF HIS
PAINTINGS   *Sunday Telegraph*

AT A FORUM ON ART   *Edward Hayes*

for 1,419 tons. Thus the output has been approximately doubled."

I'd like to bet that no journalist, editor, leading industrial correspondent or economist—or any member of the Prices and Incomes Board—can show a doubled output in service to the nation. The result of this tremendous effort, from a continuous ten-hour stint over the years up to 1964, averaging a 54-hour week (not counting a Sunday of eight hours) was that the employers were able to milk the docks industry of £178 millions, never putting a penny back into it to improve the working conditions of those who have produced that fabulous profit. And what of the cost in life and limb to the registered port worker? One man in every 1,500 killed on the job; one man in eight seriously injured; every man attended the medical centres on an average four times a year. (During my stay in hospital in 1959, when I had fallen 50 feet down a ship's hold, I went round the wards talking to injured workmates; I never got a chance to sit by the bedside of an employer broken in body trying to make a living, not even one with a strained finger from counting all those millions—they even employ others to do that for them. Back Britain! why, this bunch have never been off our backs!)

So that was the situation in 1964, the result of our endeavours, our agitation and resistance. The national delegates stood firm against all the oratory of the General Secretary and the pleas of the National Dock Groups Secretary; 19s. 2d. was achieved, and though we were 5s. 10d. short of our demand, the rest was favourably received by the rank and file.

But the London liaison committee had the feeling that this was the "sweetener" for Phase 2, where the *quid pro quo*, this for that, would be launched. We'd had their quid from them, and now from us they wanted the quo—our protective practices (the employers call them "restrictive"), manning scales, mobility, overtime practices and payments, etc.

So it was back to work to wait for the magic formula for the solution of all port problems out of Lord Devlin's hat; meanwhile, the liaison committee returned to the agitation for the nationalisation of the port industry.

On my arrival home one night after the day's work, Ellen told me that a letter had come from Lord Thompson, inviting me to speak at the Annual Dinner of the 31 Club at Claridge's Hotel.

The membership, apparently, consisted of thirty-one millionaires in the advertising and publicity business. Naturally, I was puzzled as to why I had been chosen as the guest speaker, but in a telephone conversation I was told by Lord Thompson's private secretary that it was the customary practice of the Club to invite a personality to address the Annual Dinner and Lord Thompson, being the Chairman for that year, had chosen me.

I said I would consider it, and I discussed it with Ellen, because I was concerned as to what some of my friends—and enemies— might make of it if I accepted. However, after we'd talked it over, I thought of a line in one of my favourite poems, Kipling's "If"—"Or walk with Kings—nor lose the common touch"— and decided to write to Lord Thompson saying I would come. Within a week I received a further invitation, to go to the House of Lords with Ellen and discuss the Annual Dinner over a cup of tea with Lord Thompson. I thought this would be too much. Imagine what the *Daily Mirror* would have made of that! I explained my reasons, and they were accepted; we were invited instead to go to Thompson House, the publishing headquarters.

In due course Ellen and I made the call. We were taken up by lift and welcomed by a private secretary, who informed us that Lord Thompson was making a trans-Atlantic phone call, and showed into a waiting room where there were newspapers and journals from all corners of the world. I examined them with great interest, and discovered that one important national daily was missing—the *Morning Star*. I made a mental note to raise this with Lord Thompson.

We were finally ushered in by the secretary. I shook hands with our host and greeted him with: "How you going, Roy?" In turn he called me Jack, and I introduced Ellen. The studio was spacious and light, overlooking the surrounding area, with simple furnishing in good taste. Above the fireplace there was an impressionist painting in the Renoir style. It really fascinated me, though usually I am not very keen on impressionism. I remarked that I was taken with it, and Roy asked me: "Do you know what it portrays? If you do, you'll be the only one who does, apart from one other person." Taking time to consider, I told him that the painting gave me the impression of an elephant bathing in a lily-pond. With an exclamation of excitement, he said: "That's it! And the only other person to get it right was Princess Margaret." I laughed, and said that apart from the fact that we were both members of the human race, our understanding of the picture was just about all we had in common.

He took the point in a good-natured way, quite nice and friendly like many of those I have met among the property-owning class (though when you want to separate them from their money they're as hard as brick). Roy himself is a man of small stature but tough physique, and as you get deeper into conversation with him you realise that here is a tough one. During our talk over tea and pastries we discussed the forth-coming annual dinner and the procedure. I said I hoped evening dress was "optional" because I'd be wearing a lounge suit; with a smile he said that he had never expected otherwise though all the guests would be in evening attire. On our departure I mentioned the absence of the *Morning Star* in the guests' waiting room. Lord Thompson said he would put this right, but as to whether he did your guess is as good as mine. During our tête-à-tête I was struck by the irony of the situation: here was I, talking airily to a multi-millionaire about his private village project and looking at photos of his villa in southern France, and I'd experienced three days' unemployment that same week.

On the evening of this unusual invitation, I was fetched by car to Claridge's Hotel, and as I went in, my mind went back to a previous visit to that renowned eating house. On that occasion I had been wearing a poster calling for the release of that great working-class fighter for the Greek people, Tony Ambatielos, who was serving a life sentence in one of the most terrible Greek prisons. With us had been Tony's wonderful, courageous wife Betty, known to the whole world for her valiant struggle on behalf of her husband and his fellow prisoners. We had gone to demonstrate at Claridge's because the Greek Queen was staying there and on that occasion there had been no welcoming smiles. This time, however, I was ushered into the guest room, greeted by Lord Thompson and introduced to the waiting guests (all in evening dress).

The wine waiter approached and asked what I'd like to drink. I chose a lemonade. This caused one of the millionaires to smile and remark: "A docker drinking lemonade!" I replied that I was about to enter the lions' den and must remember that "when the wine is in, the wit's out", but I'd be prepared to join him afterwards and drink the hard stuff.

We took our places in the dining room, a very resplendent job with beautiful chandeliers. On my left sat Lord Thompson, the chairman, and on my right Sir Timothy Bligh, who had been Private Secretary to the two previous Prime Ministers, Harold Macmillan and Sir Alec Douglas Home and was now Private Secretary to Lord Thompson. During dinner, we got round to talking about the forthcoming General Election, and Sir Timothy asked which political party I thought would be returned. I said I was confident that it would be the Labour Party but that his class need have no fears because Socialism was not the objective of that unholy trinity Wilson, Brown and Gunter; I realised, I said, that it was nice to wield the whip, but a Labour Cabinet would do their job equally well and the Tories wouldn't have to take the can back; and millions could continue to be made as fast as a computer could handle the count. For this I received a warm and understanding smile.

As the meal drew to its close, they asked me how long I proposed to speak on the subject of the docks. I said I would take about forty-five minutes, and was politely but strongly advised to cut it down to about twenty minutes as some of the guests would get fidgety if I went on for longer than that. However, I spoke for almost an hour, and was heard with great attention and in absolute silence, even when I was making caustic remarks about the captains of industry, the employers. At the end of the speech there was warm applause. Of the fifteen or so questions I was called on to reply to following my speech, only *one* concerned the subject on which I had been talking—the docks. The rest were about the role of the Communist Party, about the Soviet Union's pact with Nazi Germany in 1938, my individual actions as a Communist. I answered up as best I could; it was an interesting evening and I was courteously thanked for my contribution.

This event was followed by a whole series of invitations to speak and debate all over the country. I have had the pleasure of speaking at thirty-four universities, from Edinburgh and Glasgow down through the north at Durham, Hull, Liverpool and Manchester, through the Midlands to Coventry, Nottingham, Birmingham, Leeds and Leicester; at London University, Imperial College, Goldsmith's College, at Oxford (four times), Cambridge, Sussex, Swansea and Cardiff. During one of my visits to Oxford, where I have been elected an honorary Vice-President of the Oxford University Labour Club, I had the pleasure of meeting William David, Financial Editor of the

Guardian and defeating him in debate: "That this House would outlaw unofficial strikes." I also had the good fortune to meet a former Air Defence Minister of the Tory Cabinet, Mr Hugh Fraser, and defeat him in debate at Birmingham University on the subject: "Capitalism Corrupts." And quite recently, with a much narrower margin than the others, I defeated Mr H. Silverman in a debate: "That this House supports unofficial strikes." I have travelled approximately 20,000 miles to date, speaking on behalf of the rank and file of the port industry.

The Devlin Report

The London Liaison Committee renewed its campaign for the New Dockers' Charter, which was reprinted, along with 5,000 sticky-backs which read: "Don't Devlinise—Nationalise!" These were issued out to the lads, who slapped them on to cranes, P.L.A. rail trucks, the windscreens of their cars, and on the front of that seat of the London docks trade union reactionaries, Transport House, West India Dock Road.

We started our own docks newspaper—*The Docker's Voice*. It had a too-short life, mainly because of lack of salesmen; it was far too much for a committee of five both to produce it and sell it to 9,000 men. It is a great pity we had to go out of circulation, for there is a real need for a rank-and-file newspaper. There is, in fact, an industrial newspaper serving the Port of London; it is called *The Port* and is financed by the largest single employer in London, the Port of London Authority. The paper itself is produced by an independent board of journalists: independent as they all may be, this journal still conforms. Strangely enough, it never lacks support from our trade union officials; they love to write or comment in it, or pose for photographs, though they would never contribute to the rank and file press.

The Minister of Labour, Ray Gunter, released to the general public the draft amendments to the Dock Employment Scheme. Each of us on the London Liaison Committee bought a copy of it and studied it thoroughly. We found it full of threats to our working conditions and protective practices, and we felt that we'd better alert the rank and file to its dangers. I was instructed by the committee to address the men at various dock gate meetings, to spell out the terms of the proposed draft in dock language, crossing the t's and dotting the i's, showing that in its present form it would take us back to the working conditions of the days of the *Cutty Sark*, the renowned sailing clipper of the grain era. Other meetings were addressed by such capable speakers as Ernie Rice, Danny Lyons and Terry Barratt, and the "back-room boys"—the men without whom committees and campaigns cannot function—were David Timothy, Bernie Steers, Buck Baker. Our objective was to get the Minister of Labour to set up an inquiry which all interested bodies could attend, to state their proposals and objections to the draft amendments.

Our committee addressed meetings all over London. We distributed postcards to our members, calling on the Prime Minister to raise the matter with the Minister of Labour; the rank and file members bought stamps and posted them. A mass march was convened for a Sunday; a thousand men took part, with posters calling for a public enquiry and the nationalisation of the ports. The demonstration formed up at 11 a.m. under Big Ben (who again had both hands up in our favour). One of the lads made us laugh with the remark that Big Ben and Lord Nelson had attended more public meetings than anyone and never put a penny in the collections. With the usual police escort, we marched off up Whitehall to No. 10 Downing Street to deliver a big batch of signed postcards to Mr. Wilson. A police guard was stretched right across the entrance to Downing Street, and the Commissioner informed us that only a deputation of five would be permitted to enter and hand over the petitions. Five members of the committee were elected, including myself, but we informed the police chief that we would hold a meeting after calling at No. 10 to inform the men what had taken place. It was agreed that we should meet in a cul-de-sac opposite Horse Guards Parade.

Surrounded by press reporters and photographers, we knocked at the door of No. 10. But instead of meeting Harold Wilson, all we saw was a uniformed domestic. Somewhat disappointed, we handed in the petition cards with the London portworkers' demands. One of our dock wags, an inveterate joker, said the Prime Minister must be out in his back garden practising "about-turns", for in the field of politics Harold Wilson could do an about-turn smarter than any of the sentries at Buckingham Palace.

We made our way to the meeting place where the rest of the lads were waiting, and I climbed on to a window-sill which was wide enough to stand on, and through a loud-hailer told them about our reception at No. 10. While I was speaking, I was heckled by an Empire Loyalist, who kept shouting and pointing to his rows of military medals; this began to infuriate the lads, but the police acted quickly and removed the heckler for his own protection.

The meeting then dispersed, but the liaison committee crossed into St James's Park for an impromptu committee meeting with some visiting members from Bootle and Liverpool, the press standing at a distance and taking photographs while we conferred. We decided on an ultimatum. If the public enquiry was not held by a certain date, we would call for a withdrawal of labour.

This, however, was unnecessary, for the Minister of Labour shortly afterwards announced the date of a public enquiry on the proposed amendments to the Docks Employment Scheme, to be conducted under the chairmanship of Sir George Honeyman. (No doubt about it, the Establishment dearly love titled people who know nothing about the industry.)

So once again, the mass activity of the rank and file had moved the Establishment into action, and even the national press was forced to admit that it was the London Liaison Committee that had brought the whole thing before the public.

At the enquiry, the accredited trade unions attended and made known their objections: there were three objectors from the Docks Trade Group of the Transport and General Workers' Union, twenty-three (to their credit) from the National Amalgamated Stevedores and Dockers' Union, and myself and Terry Barratt from the Liaison Committee. We raised objections to pretty well all the proposals except for the amendment dealing with sick pay and pensions.

Again dock-gate meetings were mounted; a report-back meeting was held to describe our contribution to the enquiry, and a vote of confidence was registered by the rank and file in our handling of their demands.

On July 28, 1965, the whole of London's waterfront from Tilbury to the upper reaches at Brentford was seething with discussion about the future for us port workers. The reason? The long-awaited report of the Devlin Committee had been released, heralding a "golden era" that was to end all the inequalities between man and man (if you were to believe the press).

You'd have thought the millennium was about to arrive. The news boys (reporters) were covering the entire waterfront, seeking interviews with the rank and file to discover their reactions—ignoring the fact that 95 per cent of them hadn't seen a copy of the report, first because the Ministry of Labour had not seen fit to print or release more than about 2,000 copies (among 63,000 workers) and second because they were rationed by price (at 10s. per copy). Because of this the reactions of the rank and file were based mainly on the interpretations handed out by the national press.

At home, my wife was badgered by newspapermen calling to ask my opinion of the report. When they drew a blank, they came down to the Royal Group to find me. The first question they asked, once they'd tracked me down to where I was working, was: what was the Liaison Committee's view of the report and how did we see the future for dockland?

I told them politely and patiently that at this stage the Liaison Committee was in no position to make a statement, because the Report has only been in our possession for 24 hours and there had not been time to make a thorough study of it. As soon as we were able to do so, I told the press, we would meet to discuss it, and whatever recommendations we arrived at would be transmitted to the rank and file at mass meetings.

Ever impatient, they asked how soon that would be. Vicky Turner, who was with me, replied: "How soon? Why, it's taken four learned men of the Establishment nine months to arrive at their recommendations, and now you expect five working men, after doing a ten-hour stint not counting travelling time, to rush home, gollop their evening meal, and, not stopping to play with the kids—who up till the ban on weekend working thought we were the lodger—or say a word of endearment to our wives, whip out the Devlin report and start studying!"

There was laughter all round. The reporters took the point, however, and I assured them that once the committee had finally arrived at its policy, they would be contacted and informed of the date and times of the mass meetings.

After several days of conferring during our meal-breaks, and nightly after work, sometimes not getting home until ten o clock or later, we finally reached a unanimous decision. We found that the report was heavily weighted in favour of the employers and was a blueprint for cutting the labour force by a third as first

K

step to modernisation and mechanisation of the industry. We were all for making the industry efficient, but we had our own opinion on what was necessary and how it could be achieved. We are not Luddites. We are not opposed to mechanisation as such. But we are opposed to mechanisation when it puts men on the dole. As I said at the time: "Progress measured by the degree of automation you can get without considering the plight of the displaced worker is not progress at all. We welcome new techniques, but hard experience has taught us that people want us to drop our guard for the benefit of the employers, not for that of the men who work in the industry." The type of modernisation "they" seemed to want, accompanied the introduction, for instance, of fork-lift trucks into our docks: as I mentioned earlier it took six men to operate two of these trucks and they replaced seven gangs employing fifty-six men. At the same time the employers cut the general cargo rate from 3s. to 1s. 6d. a ton.

Having arriving at our constructive criticism of the Devlin Report, we decided to convene a number of mass meetings. The press, the BBC and ITV television circuits were informed, and duly covered the meetings. At the same time we resolved to publish and issue to all the national ports a broadsheet setting out our opinions on what was necessary to make an efficient port industry. Here is what we said:

CHANGES IN THE DOCKS

The Devlin Report is not just another Docks Industry report. To underestimate its importance would be folly indeed. It could be the basis for a major attack on manning scales, protective practices, working hours and conditions.

If implemented it will give the employers a much greater degree of the control of labour, and disciplinary powers to enforce their will. However it will not solve the problem of Dockland for it does not strike at the root of the troubles, i.e., the competitive, unplanned nature of the industry, and the chaotic conditions enforced on it by outside interests.

The Report has some favourable points—if they are carried out.

1. Recommendation for a higher guaranteed wage.

2. The introduction of sick and accident pay.
3. A system of shop stewards in Dockland.
4. Welfare facilities to be greatly improved.

But it also has unacceptable points.

1. The proposed permanency scheme under individual employers, and major inroads into the powers of the National Dock Labour Board.
2. The proposals for abolition of protective practices.
3. More tonnage to be handled by a smaller labour force under more intensive conditions and with no proportionate reward.

Dockers now face a twofold task:

1. To achieve maximum unity to influence and strengthen the hand of our negotiators to secure major advances in wages and working conditions.
2. To urge, press and campaign for the BASIC CHANGES needed but rejected by Devlin.

The report states that witnesses from the trade union side expressed a preference for the scheme to be "administered by the Board" and used phrases like "decasualisation under the auspices of the Board" and referred in a general way to "the advantages of administration by the Board". . . . *The overwhelming majority of the rank and file would favour such a Scheme. If such is not available at this time, far better to maintain the* status quo *than subject the labour force to the retrograde step of "weekly engagement by individual employers".*

The Broadsheet continued:

The (Devlin) Report was commissioned by the government. This in itself makes the Report a political act.

Seen alongside the National Plan it falls into place as part of a nation-wide effort to modernise Britain's industries.

In 1948 a Labour Government put the full control of labour under the National Dock Labour Board, which was responsible to the Minister and through him to Parliament.

Devlin means that the control of labour is to be handed back, to a considerable extent, to the employers.

This was never the intention of the scheme.

The National Dock Labour Board is part of the public sector of the economy, and any changes in it that lessen the power of the Trade Unions and increase the powers of private enterprise are in effect a measure of de-nationalisation.

The disease in Britain's ports will not be cured by attacks on the labour force nor resolved by a solution that sees further exploitation as the answer.

The answer lies in Point 11 of the Charter—"nationalisation of the industry". This will require Parliamentary action. Dockland M.P.'s must study the report and heed the voice of the dock-worker in the coming months, likewise local councils and councillors.

To the rank and file of dockland we say, conduct the struggle for the Charter at all levels, in the Branches, at the dock gates, through your M.P.'s, local Councillors and political parties.

Secure the support of our Trade Union officials, win the support of fellow trade unionists outside the docks, get public opinion on our side!

Besides being sent to all the national ports, the broadsheet was sent to every important figure in the corridors of power in Parliament and Transport House. Our recommendations were ignored—of course; it would have lowered their dignity to have acknowledged the opinions, the skill and intelligence that exist in the servants' quarters. Had our views been acknowledged, a major strike of nine weeks, affecting the ports of London and Liverpool, could have been avoided.

Every mass meeting was well attended. The findings and recommendations of the London Liaison Committee were overwhelmingly supported. In the meantime, news reports of the *Daily Express*, in their thirst for something sensational, had interpreted a statement made by Lord Devlin in the report concerning what he called "wreckers" as referring to me. Naturally, I took a strong objection to being named as a wrecker, and sought legal advice. My solicitor advised me to complain to the Press Council —whose Chairman at that time, incidentally, was Lord Devlin himself. In due course the *Express* was informed that I was not to be named as a wrecker, and within a few days it printed an apology. However, I must say that with the exception of a couple of other clashes (one with the *Daily Telegraph* and a second one with the *Daily Express*) my relationship with news-reporters, industrial correspondents and journalists has been of the friendliest; the only ones towards whom I feel anger and disgust at some of their reports concerning myself are those of the *Daily Mirror* group, who have attempted to assassinate my character with a journalese that is lower than low—but more about that later.

During the Devlin campaign and the discussion of our broadsheet, we lobbied the dockside M.P.'s and it was arranged that we should be specially received in a committee room one evening in order to discuss port matters. On the evening we were courteously received by the Members for Dagenham—Mr Parker; for Poplar—Ian Mikardo; and for my own borough of Stepney— a Wilson protege, a university type, later to become Cabinet Minister, Peter Shore who, during the course of the discussion confessed that he was unaware of the mass unemployment that was being experienced on Stepney's waterfront.

However, after keen questioning and discussion, we adjourned with the usual vague and negative promises from the professional politicians, all very statesmanlike and diplomatic, but saying lots and meaning nothing, leaving us empty-handed and disappointed.

Over a cup of tea in the nearby Corner House, I remarked: "The quicker we return a few Communist M.P.'s to Parliament the better. It would be like having a Liaison Committee amongst the Labour benches, a militant ginger-group to bring the left-wing shadow boxers down to earth and face them with reality." This led to a discussion concerning the dockside M.P.'s, members of the Transport and General Workers' Union, who were at that time in receipt of an annual payment from the Union yet never raised a peep in the House on behalf of their union brothers and dockside constituents. From there we went on to talk about the full-time Transport and General Workers' Union officials who sit on the National and London Dock Labour Boards. They have two hats, said someone—they go into Board meetings wearing their dockers' cloth caps, which they hang up in the cloakroom and don their official bowlers to discuss the port industry and its problems in a genteel manner with their joint members, the employers' representatives. I have heard that our General Secretary Frank Cousins, at a meeting with the Board officials during this very period, told them in no uncertain terms to remember that they weren't members of the Board but trade union representatives of the men, *jointly* sitting with the employers; but it didn't seem to have had much effect.

We took leave of each other that night more firmly convinced than ever that nothing short of a revolution would bring about the socialist nationalisation of the port industry, and until that was done our industry would continue from one year to another with all the inefficiency and antiquated methods of work that stem from private ownership (which still continues to make millions of profit). Talk about patriotism! Quite recently an order to build five modern ships to operate the revolution of cargo-handling, containerisation, was placed—in Britain? a nation with the finest shipbuilding skills in the whole world? Don't kid yourself!—in Japan. Back Britain? That's only for the proles, well-meaning young office-girls and misguided factory workers.

19

The Liaison Committee

Let me introduce you, dear reader, to some of those members (past and present) of the Liaison Committee, the men who have built it into such an important voice of London's port workers, known throughout the British labour movement and even in the farthest corners of the Commonwealth; a committee that has publicly stated that it is not in existence to usurp the power of our accredited trade unions but to urge and persuade the rank and file to be alert and active as trade unionists, to attend their branches regularly, to formulate policies and see that they are carried out.

We are an elected body, and our method of work is to make recommendations for progressive aims and objectives to be won at branch level; this we do by means of dock-gate meetings and leaflets. If no heed is paid to the men's demands by the official trade union leadership, we call mass meetings and propose mass action. The success of the unofficial Docks Liaison Committee has been won because we are a day-to-day living part of the rank and file, working side by side, sharing the good times and the hard ones, the long hours of back-breaking toil at piecework speed, listening to and taking part in the grumbles and grouses of our fellow-workers: this is the reason for the respect we have won. When we speak at meetings it is not in a Transport House-cultured voice, using statesmanlike terms: we talk dock language: there is no division of us and them, we *are* them.

So here are some sketches of those who have unstintingly sacrificed their leisure-time and meal-hours on behalf of their fellow-workers, often getting into heated arguments and some-times boiling over, because you can't be all things to all men.

Meet Vicky Turner, young, married, with a family, shrewd and intelligent, with a personality that is alight with humour, fond of making a "funny" (a pun). One of Vicky's characteristics is the way he gestures with his forefinger; the more intense and heated he becomes in argument, the more violent become the emphatic gestures of that pointing index. This is why he is often referred to as "Fingers" Turner, to distinguish him from all the other Turners in the Royal Group of docks—and you can bet we have more turners than a machine shop in a factory. During the "Devlin" period, when elections were held for trade union branch lay officials, we of the Liaison Committee advised Vicky to accept nomination, because we were confident that he would serve the rank and file in a positive and skilful manner and because, as a branch official, he would be an almost automatic choice to represent Branch No. 1/37, the most militant branch on London's waterfront, on the divisional committee. Vicky was reluctant to leave the Liaison Committee, on which he had served so well. But being a good militant trade unionist, he accepted our decision and in due course was nominated and overwhelmingly elected as the new Chairman of 1/37, becoming divisional delegate of his branch, and divisional committee delegate to the Ocean Shipowners' Joint Group Committee, where he has made his presence strongly felt—much to the sorrow of the employers. Throughout the bitterest struggles and strikes he has stood firm and challenged on behalf of the men (some-times as a lone rider, which takes guts). Vicky has recently been elected to a most important committee that will be attempting to plan the future of London's registered port workers—the London Modernisation Committee—and with a man of his calibre and sincerity sitting there on our behalf, I am confident that the employers will be faced with a resolute and formidable opponent.

Ernie Rice, short of stature but tough, in his middle-forties, married with a family, has been a member of the Liaison Com-mittee only for a short time; but he has been a great asset to it because of his very precise, methodical handling of industrial documents. He was the initiator of the Royal Group wall-newspaper. As a result of working in the refrigerated holds of meat-carrying ships, his health is impaired and he finds it difficult to sleep. He would stay up half the night, working with coloured pens to produce posters with vividly-presented factual infor-mation concerning agreements, sick pay, severance pay, the proposals of the London Modernisation Committee concerning

"GOOD MORNING, BROTHERS!" FEBRUARY 1968

Press Association

A PORTWORKER
ON THE JOB
Pat Mante

"WHAT CHANCE WOULD I HAVE TO KID LADS OF SUCH CALIBRE?"
Morning Sta

decasualisation and all manner of other subjects of vital concern. These posters are eagerly studied by the rank and file, creating tremendous discussions—and often causing searching questions to be put to the paid trade union officials. Since joining the Liaison Committee he has developed into a very capable speaker.

Next comes big Wally Harris, young, heavily built, red-haired, ruddy-complexioned, married with a family. Wally is very quick on working out percentages and is fearless in facing any opposition, no matter what is the calibre or reputation of his opponents. He doesn't bother with finesse, but calls the score as he sees it and sticks strongly to his point of view; but if, after discussion, he is convinced that he's been wrong, he's quick to admit it and accept the decisions of the committee. On the recommendation of the Liaison Committee, on which he had given fine service, Wally too accepted branch nomination and was duly elected by 1/37 Branch, to join Vicky Turner as a divisional representative, where he has made his formidable presence strongly felt.

David Timothy, in his early 30's, is the son of the late Albert Timothy—"Timmo", one of the seven dockers arrested during the struggle against Clause 1305 (see Chapter 10). David, unlike his fiery father, is quietly-spoken and even tempered, until put out when he can become aggressive and determined in his point of view. He was elected our Treasurer, and has been a thoroughly admirable guardian of our funds, with an account book that has always stood up to the keenest of auditing. Always reliable, is David.

Danny Lyons, five feet ten inches, with a thick unruly shock of hair, is in his mid-forties, a family man, with a deeply thoughtful person. He has a slight tendency to speak in a didactic manner, though not in an egotistical vein. He has been elected a member of the executive committee of the British Communist Party, and has considerable ability as an orator.

Roy Tierney served on the Liaison Committee through its most severe tribulations and trials, and developed into an excellent pamphleteer. Deeply sincere and self-sacrificing on behalf of his fellow workers, a family man and a branch secretary of the "Blue" union, he had the misfortune to be stricken with cardiac trouble and was forced to retire from active militancy.

Jimmy Lear, of a very athletic physique, is in his 30's, a teacher of unarmed combat and a qualified teacher of motor mechanics at evening classes. Always humorous, he is very hard-working and a first-rate committee man. When he is in his cups he carries on a non-stop Irish jig; this is probably because of his Irish lineage.

Johnny Madget, married with a family, is in his 40's. He would put his car at the disposal of the committee whenever it was needed, without a moment's hesitation. He's apt to get emotional when angry or disturbed, but when he's on an even keel he's a very reliable person.

During the docks de-casualisation campaign, two new members came on to the committee, both of them youngsters. Micky Finn, in his 20's, is married, with a family, and extremely intelligent. With all the impatience of youth, he is inclined to be excitable; but as the weeks of the strike wore on he gained experience and learned from it; he's a good asset for the future. Alan Cunningham, young and single, is a great reader; one of his favourite subjects is psychology and because when he gets on to that subject he's practically unstoppable, the lads often refer to him as "the head-shrinker". Alan has just been awarded a certificate of merit by the union for a study course on trade unionism, with an opportunity to go on to a university.

It would be unpardonable not to mention Freddie Rolfe, a valiant stalwart of the Royal Group rank and file, a deeply-respected member of the National Amalgamated Stevedores' and Dockers' Union and a member of the highest committee representing the dockers' section—a policy-making committee. Quiet-voiced, a patient listener, he is slow to anger, like most big men, but formidable once he is roused. His points of view on policy are notably objective, unsectarian on matters concerning either the docker or stevedore sections of his union.

The West India Dock Liaison Committee has been ably served by its secretary, Terry Barratt, who is short, volatile and somewhat emotional. Bernie Steers, his Chairman, is a young stevedore, a family man and a Communist; his disposition is quiet, but when the chairmanship was vacated by Buck Baker, Bernie filled the breach very adequately and developed into a fine docks orator; he is also playing a strong part in the leadership of the G.L.C. tenants' rent struggles. Harry Walker, another family man, is strongly class conscious and has developed into an excellent orator.

Such are the men I serve and have served with on the Royal Docks Liaison Committee. How many times have I smiled to myself when I've read items in the national press that try to make the public believe that it's a one-man committee, that I was the sole maker of policy; that all Jackie Dash had to do was dictate, and what I said was automatically accepted!

What chance would I have to kid lads of such calibre as these? Why, if Harold Wilson himself sat on our committee, he couldn't con them—and he's the greatest man in the con business! "Kidology?" No, each committee member has had to fight tooth and nail for the adoption of his point. These boys know all the jigs and reels.

20

The Campaign

We continued our meetings, spelling out the dock phraseology what the Report would mean to our working conditions, holding forth down ships' holds, on the quayside, at the wharves and warehouses. In order to comply with the Devlin Report, the National Joint Council had agreed to restore the National Amalgamated Stevedores' & Dockers' Union to the participation from which it had been excluded since 1936. This was welcomed as a progressive step, but it was virtually negated by an agreement, reached in September 1965, that in effect bound the unions to reveal no information to their members until all agreements on decasualisation had been finalised and accepted. Democracy—don't be so naive! That's something that exists in Greek history books or government speeches, all part of the great "con".

Another outcome of the Devlin Report was the formation of the National Modernisation Committee, which then gave birth to a number of separate Modernisation Committees for individual ports, which were to reach decisions in line with the custom and practice of the ports concerned. As chairman of the London Modernisation Committee, the Minister of Labour appointed Lord Brown; the Committee consisted of employers and trade union officials with three "independent" members, to be responsible for wages, sick benefits and pensions. This was Phase 1. Each port Committee was to be responsible for working practices and agreements, with special regard to our protective practices (always referred to by both employers and Ministry as "restrictive" practices). All agreements, however, had to be referred to the National Modernisation Committee. So the respective committees went merrily on their way discussing everything—the past, the present and the future—but never once consulting the mechanics, those whose knowledge and skill was based on practical experience.

The first of the plans emanating from the National Modernisation Committee was the new amended Dock Regulation of Employment Order, referred to as the New Scheme, contained in the Docks' & Harbour Bill that was placed before Parliament in 1966, with the optimistic view that if an agreement could be reached on all phases of de-casualisation, then the Decasualisation Scheme could operate in the year of its introduction. The customary ninety days were allowed so that interested persons or parties could make known their objections. The Ministry of Labour set up a commission of enquiry under the chairmanship of Sir George Honeyman.

The London Liaison Committee studied the plan in detail and again called mass meetings to spell it out to every man, dotting every i and crossing every t so that the lads should be under no illusions as to the attack on our working practices and discipline. We urged them to attend their trade union branches and put forward their objections, prepare amendments, and demand that their trade unions attend the enquiry and make known their point of view.

Approximately 200 objections were dealt with in the enquiry. They came from individual dockers from all parts of the country, from organisations connected with the industry or concerned with the interest of dock workers. My own party, the Communist Party, made a contribution that was way ahead of those of other organisations—including the trade unions—because it not only raised objections but proposed and clearly showed the need for the nationalisation of the docks as a step towards bringing about the removal of the malignant growth of inefficiency and maladministration, incurable under private enterprise.

Terry Barratt, our secretary, and I both attended on behalf of the Liaison Committee and made known the views of the men as expressed at the dock-gate mass meetings. A delegate conference was organised by the trade unions concerned, at which the employers' proposals concerning sick pay, pensions and severance pay for our aged members were made known. Because of the vigilance of the Liaison Committee, we were able to show that the terms of the sick pay scheme meant that the employers would have had to pay the proposed £6 only in very few cases and that the pensions offer did not take years of past service into consideration. This in turn caused innumerable trade union branches to call for the proposals to be sent back to the employers for further consideration.

Parallel with all this, our lay officials (elected delegates from the trade union branches) were putting up a strong fight against the attempts of the employers to introduce changes in our existing work practices agreements, particularly their attack on the Continuity Rule which has always been a thorn in their side since its inception and which we regard as our most cherished protective rule. Great credit must be given to such men as Vicky Turner, Wally Harris and Billy Knight of the No. 2 Docks Divisional Committee, Freddie Rolfe, Sectional Committee representative of the National Amalgamated Stevedores and Dockers, and to Ernie Rice for the clear and painstaking explanations on the sick pay, pensions and severence pay scheme he produced for the Liaison Committee's wall-newspaper, which was read and studied daily by thousands.

In March 1967 it was announced that the benefit proposed for the sick pay scheme was to be paid without regard to National Health benefit. This was a victory, though there was no extension of the number of benefit weeks such as we had demanded. It was also announced that agreement had been reached as to the amount to be paid as a " London weighting allowance" (for the high cost of living in the metropolis). It was to be £2 0s. 0d. We members of the Liaison Committee had a sneaking feeling that the London Modernisation Committee had really tried to bring our guaranteed earnings within striking distance of the £18 0s. 0d. we had been agitating for over the years. But wait!—the £2 0s. 0d. was not to be paid to the piece worker who had earned over £17 0s. 0d. And when permission was sought from the Minister of Labour to pay the £2 0s. 0d., he stated that this would cut across the policy of the Prices and Incomes Board, and he could only give his consent to a differential of £1 0s. 0d. for London (as recommended in the Devlin Report). In spite of the fact that it was the declared policy of the Transport & General Workers' Union to reject any interference with a freely-negotiated settlement, and that this had been negotiated by the London Docks' Group, the Union kicked up no fuss and meekly accepted Ray Gunter's dictatorial interference.

Now, as far back as May an agreement had been reached between the Advisory Committee representing the ocean ships' tally-clerks and the employers for a guaranteed week's pay of £21 1s. 8d. By summer the clerical section was getting restive, demanding that a date be set for the commencement of this new scheme and declaring that if this were not done they would withdraw their services. A withdrawal of labour by the ocean ships' tally-clerks, because of their importance to the employers and to the piece-work gangs, would have brought the whole Port of London to a standstill. The Minister of Labour panicked, set the date for the commencement of the scheme, and announced September 15th as D-day (Decasualisation Day). This was a Friday, and the date was subsequently changed, on advice, to Monday, September 18th.

The National Modernisation Committee consequently began to press for a tremendous speeding up by all the negotiating parties at every committee level. The London trade union lay delegates, who had been contesting every demand put forward by the employers with great care were informed that June 9, 1967, was the deadline for them to reach agreement—the alternative was that a decision would be reached *for* them at a higher level. The document known as the London Enclosed Docks' Agreement was hastily signed before all outstanding obstacles had been removed. Democratic procedure—the right of the rank and file to evaluate the scheme point by point and vote for acceptance or rejection on the basis of their practical skills and knowledge of the industry—was completely ignored. The Liaison Committee advocated that there should be a drive in the trade union branches for a reversal of this policy. But at the No. 2 Dock's Divisional meeting, after a report from the official platform, with keen discussion and questions, the members were told that there could be no reversal, the agreement had been signed and sealed.

You can imagine the reaction! The Liaison Committee immediately began to plan and organise resistance to this act of dictatorship. We issued leaflets, held mass dock-gate meetings, paid visits to the outer ports, endeavouring to bring about a concerted effort to halt the introduction of the Decasualisation Scheme.

I must emphasise that the Liaison Committee was not, repeat *not*, being Luddite-minded—as the general public had been led to believe by the whole of the press, radio and TV (with the significant exception of the *Morning Star*). We were in no way opposed to the Decasualisation Scheme: what we resented were its

terms. We are all for technological advance; but we want machines to save the labour of *all*, not to bestow leisure with wealth
upon the few and leisure with poverty on the many.

After trying every possible way, tackling every conceivable
responsible committee and person to press for the reversal of the
too-hasty introduction of the scheme, and failing to get common
sense to prevail, the Liaison Committee started a "count-down"
on our dock-gate wall newspaper, with daily meetings. Zero
was Friday, September 15th, and on that date the Liaison Committee met to prepare for the Monday, the 18th, the starting date,
when we were to call for a withdrawal of labour.

Precisely at eight o'clock on the Monday morning—dawn of the
new era, the promised land of the Devlin Report—I opened the
dock-gate meeting, supported by Ernie Rice and Danny Lyons.
Between us, we drew the attention of the men to the way we of
the rank and file had been conned. The inequalities which the
Report was supposed to have put an end to were still there—
indeed, they had been widened by the new pay structure. Our
brothers the ocean ships' tally-clerks would be in receipt of
£21 1s. 8d. for a forty-hour week provided they proved each
morning for employment, whether employed or not. Good luck
to them, they deserved it! Our brothers of the Watermen's,
Lightermen's & Tugmen's Union, a very old craft union, would
get £17 5s. od. for a forty-hour week and the same amount for a
five-day week of unemployment provided they proved for work.
No resentment from the dockers and stevedores at this either. But
now for the crunch: we, the piece workers, who far outnumbered
the clerks and lightermen, with our colossal piece-work output
on ten-hour stints at breakneck speed (and until we'd done this
nobody could get paid, not even the employers) were to receive the
magnificent sum of £15 0s. od.—and on top of this both the day-
worker and the piece worker were required to do three nights'
overtime until 7 p.m., the overtime payment included in the
guarantee of £15 0s. od.

What a con! The ending of inequalities, indeed, and our basic
pay still only £11 1s. 8d. Throughout the period of negotiation
during the latter half of 1967, we had demanded that the minimum basic should be £17 0s. od. A resolution for the withdrawal
of labour was put, and a majority vote was recorded in support
for this action.

We stayed out only four days. The demand that the £17 0s. od.

should be made the minimum wage was refused by the Minister of Labour, and obviously the employers would not agree that the £2 0s. 0d. weighting allowance should be part of the basic wage, since this would mean an increase in piece-work earnings equivalent to the percentage increase in the basic minimum. Our strike did not extend to the rest of the Port of London, and the Liaison Committee, after hours of deliberation, reluctantly decided to convene another meeting and recommend a return to work, rather than have a few thousand men, mainly in the Royal group of docks, isolated on the altar of sacrifice. The decision to return was unhappily accepted by a majority vote.

The Liverpool lads had also withdrawn their labour. They were going from strength to strength with grim determination. In London, the employers were cock-a-hoop because of the abortive strike, and were under the impression that the men had returned with their tails between their legs and that the Liaison Committee was no longer a force.

We had been back at work for about four days when one of the employers decided to issue a challenge, and rushed in to operate the clauses introduced in the Enclosed Docks' Agreement (known as the Grey Book, the agreement which had been signed by the trade union officials without first submitting it to the men for acceptance or rejection). In the opinion of the men, these clauses negated all the guarantees of the old Continuity Rule, and the six gangs involved withdrew their labour and placed themselves on unofficial strike. Contrary to the story as given out by the propaganda of the national press, the London Liaison Committee was unaware of what was happening until some hours later, when two members of the striking gang found where I was and came to tell me what had happened; they said that the London employers were holding a meeting in the City to consider the situation. I advised the men to go and return to their place of work and stand by, awaiting information from the City. Meanwhile, as chairman, I would get in touch with the members of the Liaison Committee and work out a line of action. We agreed to convene a dock-gate meeting and place the matter before the men. At eight o'clock the following morning we were at the dock gate, waiting for news, when we saw a well-respected trade union official, John Madden. I asked him what had happened at the City meeting, and he told us that the employers were absolutely adamant about their right to use the clauses around the Continuity Rule, and

L

refused to budge from this position. My committee instructed me to get up and address the men, describing the situation and asking them to go to their places of work and act as delegates to bring everybody out to attend a mass meeting at 10 a.m. This they did. At 10 a.m. approximately 7,000 men were in attendance. After opening the meeting, I called on one of the members of the gangs on strike to tell them at first hand exactly what had taken place. There were questions and answers, and then one after another Ernie Rice, Danny Lyons and I spoke about the threat this meant to our future, about the undemocratic negotiation and the agreement that had been signed between the trade unions and the employers.

A vote was called, for a mass withdrawal of labour in support of the gangs already on strike. A forest of hands shot up, nobody looking around to see how the other chap was voting. It was an overwhelming majority. But I went through the customary procedure, which was to call those who had abstained to come forward. Then I called again for a show of hands, and asked the abstainers to record the vote. I have never yet counted a vote at a mass meeting. Of course the press had to rush in and report that Jack Dash had made three attempts to get the vote of support—making it look as though I was hell-bent to get the stoppage.

So there it was: within four days of resuming work, it was once more into the breach, dear friends.

That same evening the Liaison Committee held a meeting to decide the next line of action: Ernie with his minute-book and pen, methodical as ever, and when he sets about recording a meeting you can bet all the tea in China that he won't miss a trick. By his side sat David Timothy, the Treasurer, looking worried at the smallness of our funds. Next to me was Danny Lyons, nonchalant as usual but deeply worried down inside. Of our two new additions to the Committee, Micky Fenn was afire with the impatience of youth and Alan Cunningham was quiet and thoughtful. We awaited the arrival of the members of the West India Dock Committee—whose membership had been reduced to two due to the departure of the other two to work at Tilbury; however, nobody is indispensable, and the working class will aways throw up leaders; young Bernie Steers and Harry Walker had filled the breach admirably.

On their arrival we all got down to business. It was decided that Harry and Bernie would convene a meeting at West India

Dock, where Ernie Rice and I would state the case and Bernie would call on the men to decide what to do. And—to get a bit ahead of my story—despite repeated attempts by the paid officials of the trade unions to confuse the men by calling meetings just before or just after ours, playing on misplaced loyalties and making a mockery of democracy by their interpretation of it, 75 per cent of the West India Dock lads gave solid support throughout the eight weeks of the struggle.

Now, I have always held the view that once men have taken the serious decision to strike, they must be closely involved in what follows, everyone taking part in picketing and in demonstrating to the public their demands and the reason for their action. So I proposed to the Committee that we should organise a march from the Royal Group, link up with our brothers in the West India Dock, march past the West India Dock Transport House (seat of reaction) and then on to Tower Hill to address the public; we should then go by Underground to the headquarters of the Labour Party and the Transport & General Workers' Union; there we would seek an interview with Frank Cousins our General Secretary and his able and very popular aide-de-camp, Jack Jones. From thence we would go in search of the Minister of Labour, Ray Gunter—and believe me, we always found Ray more elusive than the Scarlet Pimpernel.

The Liaison Committee agreed enthusiastically. The local police Superintendent was informed of our intention, and on the following morning at nine o'clock the lads from the Royal Group formed up under police escort and began the long trek to West India Dock. There were plenty of men in their sixties, plenty of middle-aged ones, and a large contingent of young ones, some a bit self-conscious since this was their first strike and public demonstration—but as the procession grew longer and wider they lost their shyness and were soon taking part in the slogan-shouting with enthusiasm. Many of them were walking side by side with their dads, beginning to realise, perhaps, some of the hardships their fathers had endured to provide for the family and rear them into manhood. It was a family march—and those of us who weren't actual blood-kin were bound in the finest brotherhood of man, the trade union movement. Right in front with the committee was an old stevedore, soon due to retire and suffering from arthritis. We were all proud of him. Every time I advised him to slow down, "Jack", he said, "this is my day. I've only a year or two left and this will be something to look back on when I'm sitting in the park thinking about years gone by". At that I held my counsel, and let him have his moment.

We reached Canning Town, turned left for the West India Dock and marched over Canning Town bridge among the heavy road-haulage, the buses and the City commuters in their private cars. As we went through Blackwall Tunnel we passed an old tramp, very dirty and unkempt, who watched us go by as he stood drinking tea out of a bottle. Pausing between swallows, he shouted: "Where are you marching to?" "Poplar Baths!" was the quick rejoinder from David Tierney. With that the old tramp nearly choked on a mouthful of tea, amid great laughter and cries of "Soap! Daz!" The jubilant mood was still high as we passed the Poplar Hospital, giving three hearty cheers for the nurses who stood on a balcony waving and smiling. Even the police escort had lost some of their formality and were exchanging cracks in the spirit of the occasion.

Our grand old stevedore was still proudly leading as we turned into High Street Poplar, a working-class borough with a proud history of industrial struggle under such leaders as Ben Tillett, Tom Mann, John Burns and George Lansbury (who with other Labour councillors went to prison for protesting against an increase in the local rates: I reckon if old George knew how this present Cabinet was performing he'd turn over in his grave with disgust).

Finally we approached the West India Docks. Lined up on either side of the road stood hundreds of the West India Dock lads, clapping and cheering. They formed in behind us as we marched on to the local Transport House; as we passed, angry shouts were directed at the windows and though the officials weren't looking out I think they could not have failed to hear such epithets as "Collaborators!" "Bosses' men!". At the dock gates the loudspeakers were waiting, and thousands of men. We made a short statement, and told the lads to make their own way to Tower Hill for the main meeting which was to take place at eleven o'clock.

Exactly on time, a gathering of approximately 3,000 registered port workers from the strike-bound sectors gathered at Tower Hill, mingled with hundreds of members of the general public, including foreign tourists, and building and road-workers from adjacent sites. I opened the meeting, introducing Danny Lyons and Ernie Rice, both of whom made very clear and factual statements. While they were speaking, my thoughts became very whimsical. I have spoken many times at this historic spot and seldom fail to think of the courageous people—noble, priest and peasant—who have been beheaded on this spot for daring to challenge the Establishment of their day for the rights of the individual, for freedom of expression and action. And about 600 yards behind is the Traitors' Gate: I thought of certain officials and of how they would blush if they stopped to read the history written above it on a plaque.

Our meeting was of short duration, because we had still much to do. Having given directions to the lads, the Liaison Committee made its way to Westminster Underground Station, and at the foot of Big Ben we marshalled the demonstration, by now 4,000 strong, with posters and banners. Exactly on the noon hour, with Big Ben's hands both bolt upright in our favour, we marched off—past the House of Commons, acknowledging the statue of another unofficial leader who challenged the Establishment successfully—Oliver Cromwell; past Millbank Gardens, with the famous masterpiece of Rodin, "The Burghers of Calais", symbol that there are humans who do not live for themselves alone. We swung right into Smith Square, the traffic at a standstill, held up by our police escort, thousands of trade unionists of the highest principles, marching with a dignity and discipline that gave the lie to those poisonous headlines in the (then) Cecil King press that sought to show the dockers as bloody-minded, selfish and arrogant. Selfish? Here were the men who had stopped work to show their sympathy and support for the State Registered Nurses' plea for an increase in their meagre salaries. Was that the action of selfish, bloody-minded men?

We lined up beneath a block of offices opposite Transport House, shouting—roaring, "Clauses in, we're out!". The Committee was about to enter Transport House to lobby Jack Jones when an ugly incident occurred which might have led to trouble. A well-mannered, pardon-me-chaps office worker threw a cup of tea down amongst the men, from about five floors up, narrowly missing hurting anyone. There were cries of rage, and a rush towards the building, which might well have ended in a smash-up. The Committee, and police close on our heels, acted quickly, headed them off and made strong appeals for discipline and a refusal to be provoked. The lads conceded. The police, who knew how explosive the situation had become, thanked us and went into the office block to investigate.

Meanwhile we, the Committee, went into Transport House to parley with Jack Jones. To our disappointment, we were informed that both he and T. O'Leary, the national officers, had gone to Ray Gunter, the Minister of Labour.

We informed the lads of the situation. With one united roar: "On to the Ministry of Labour!" they formed themselves into threes without any marshalling, and off we set, under police escort—spirits still high, and every mini-skirted London sight-seer receiving admiring glances and wolf-whistles. As the demonstration passed the end of Downing Street, there was a police cordon stretched across the entrance. But except that the slogans were shouted in louder voices (and one or two Bronx cheers) there was no incident.

Through Trafalgar Square we went, passing that most consistent attender at mass meetings, Lord Nelson, and along Pall Mall where club members came to their windows to see who was breaking their silence rules ("Some of the best-dressed out-of-works I've ever seen", remarked one of ours). Turning into St James' Square, with everyone in good voice, we finally arrived outside the Ministry of Labour. At the request of the police, we called on our lads to stand well back and allow the cars and taxis to pass. The liaison committee, accompanied by the six delegates from Liverpool who had joined us at Tower Hill entered the building to seek an interview with Ray Gunter. We were courteously received by a clerk who took in our request, but after about ten minutes came back to say that the Minister was attending the House, but if we left a statement in writing, it would be handed to him. We prepared a statement, and the Liverpool brothers drew one up concerning their own problems. Then we went outside, read out the statement, called for a vote, which was unanimously in favour, and saw the Private Secretary in his office, who promised to hand the statement to the Minister himself.

When we got outside again, there was a strong demand from the men that we should march back to Transport House and try to see Jack Jones—the one man, outside of Frank Cousins, for whom they had a real warm regard. So without further ado we formed up again and began the return journey, to the tune—as we turned back into Smith Square—of *Here we Are Again!* Again we were unable to see J. L. Jones, but this time we were received by the national Docks' secretary, T. O'Leary, O.B.E., and the London Docks' Group secretary, Peter Shea, with the lay members of the Docks' Group Committee. Although we were received politely, the air was chill, for we were now facing the men who had agreed to the Enclosed Docks' Employment Agreement before mass meetings of the rank and file had had a chance to accept or reject it.

As chairman of the Liaison Committee, I made the opening statement, and was followed by others of the delegation. A reply was given by Peter Shea and there were contributions from the lay officials. Meanwhile, smoking a long cheroot, sat the National Docks' Secretary looking aloof and nonchalant; and after the final contribution from his side, he made a summing-up. There was a lot of stuff about using and honouring the constitutional procedure of committees from the branches upwards (which was teaching Grandma how to suck eggs) and no action could be taken until there was a full return to work. He finished up with some platitudes about socialism and democracy; it was like an address from a Roman Senator to the plebians and proles. We thanked the Docks' Group Committee, told them we would make known their recommendations at our next mass meeting, and departed to inform the lads outside. Our report was greeted with many kinds of four-letter words, some of which were even new to me.

A few mornings later we read in the press that our General Secretary Frank Cousins had cut short his visit to the United States and was to return to look into the issues of London and Liverpool. The Liverpool lads had now entered their fifth week of strikes, and we were in our third. It was about this time that the Cecil King group, through the columns of the *Daily Mirror* (the navvies' comic) began an attempt to assassinate my character. Unfortunately, a terrible tragedy had befallen us: one of our mates, Terry Murphy, veteran of many unofficial strikes and a member of a very militant dock family, committed suicide. A news reporter, taking advantage of his widow's distress and emotional strain, had put it to her that Jack Dash and the unofficial strike were the cause. No doubt it was the shock and grief which made her agree. Next day there appeared photographs of Mrs Murphy and myself, side by side, with the headline "Mrs Murphy Blames Jack Dash and the Unofficial Leaders for her

Husband's Death". I have no printable words to describe this piece of *journalism*, which set in motion a stream of abusive telephone calls to Ellen, my wife, concerning me, her husband. Some were accompanied by threats of physical violence, and there were letters also—of course, unsigned. One evening during the strike, I was disturbed in the writing of this autobiography by a knock at the door. I opened it, to find two fine specimens of six-foot manhood, and before they had time to announce themselves I hazarded a guess that they were police officers. They were; from Scotland Yard. I invited them in; they informed me that Scotland Yard had received telephone calls informing them that I was going to be shot. They were therefore offering to arrange police protection if I so desired. I thanked them, but declined, saying I was quite sure that if anyone really intended to make an attack on my life, the last thing they'd do would be to inform the police. They agreed, but said it was the duty of the police, once having been informed, to offer police protection as a precaution. Thank goodness Ellen was out visiting our daughter when this happened; otherwise she would have spent many anxious hours during my absence.

The father and one of the brothers of poor Terry Murphy were so upset and angry at the report in the *Daily Mirror* that they made a personal visit to the News Editor, to deny that Terry's act was a result of the strike and saying that they themselves were 100 per cent in support of it.

But there! This is only one of the brushes we have had with the *Mirror* clan since 1961 and through the Devlin era. London's dock workers have been constant victims of their abusive and insulting headlines ("Dockers are Bloody-Minded, Arrogant and Selfish"—*Sunday Mirror*), the purpose being to arouse the general public against us for not doing more than a fifty-hour week. This last headline was followed by what the *Sunday Mirror* admitted was "an avalanche of letters" from dockers and others, which forced it to admit that: "At the root of the trouble are penny-pinching bosses, clumsy and wasteful handling of labour and antiquated machinery" . . . but still no apology. At least the *Daily Mirror* is now honest enough no longer to carry the slogan: "Forward with the People".

21

The Strike

The London Liaison Committee, after many hours of discussion, reached the conclusion that the strike could no longer be contained in the Royal Group and the West India Dock (who were supporting us in spite of continuous right-wing attacks from the local Transport House). To extend the struggle, therefore, it was decided to visit the Tilbury sector, to state our case, and then leave it for discussion by the Tilbury Liaison Committee. We were told that the committee had not been functioning actively for some time; no doubt this was because their popular Chairman, Charlie Cole, had left the industry to manage a pub. Undaunted, we went to Tilbury and saw Terry Barratt, who had formerly been secretary of the West India Dock liaison committee but had been transferred to the Tilbury sector, where he was still very much a "new boy". Because of its distance from the Port of London, Tilbury could well be a port in its own right, and because of this, it has not been so closely involved in the London post-war struggles; the Tilbury men have taken care of their own problems in a fashion satisfactory to themselves. Shall I say, then, that Terry was still finding it a bit "parochial". Nevertheless he managed to induce a couple of hundred men to leave a nearby pub for an impromptu meeting to hear the issue stated by their London brothers. I stated the issue, standing on a chair. Terry then asked them to come back the next day when the London committee would be there in force. On the following day our Committee arrived to find a meeting of about 800 men. Terry Barratt opened the meeting. Immediately a small group of about fifteen men began to barrack, implying that he was an intruder among them; among the most vociferous of these was a lay official of the London Docks' Group who had been party to the agreement that had caused the strike; he wanted to prevent

London from having a hearing. After announcing me as the next speaker. Terry got down. I then attempted to outline our reasons for being on strike, but was given no chance by the noisy group who were there to make sure that the Tilbury men would not get a chance to listen. After a ten-minute attempt, I got down; scores of Tilbury men came over to apologise for the behaviour of the hecklers and to commiserate with me. Naturally I was disappointed, but I was not angry or vindictive, for the very fact that some 800 men had stopped work, losing an hour's pay, proved that they wanted to listen but had been prevented from doing so. Of course the national press made capital out of it. "Unofficial Strike Leader Shunned by the Men of Tilbury", "London Dockers Turned Away" . . .

Our next visit was to Sector 6 of the London Dock area; this time we led a march, but when we reached London dock the men were all at work. However, we were met by the official Shop Stewards' Committee, under the chairmanship of Harry Wilcox, who after listening to our case, promised to convene a mass meeting to hear us. He kept his word, and at 8 a.m. on the following Wednesday the meeting was held—amid a block of flats with housewives standing on the balconies, many of them doubtless—and who could blame them—cursing the disturbance of the breakfast-table peace and any little ones still sleeping. In attendance was the London Docks' Group secretary, Peter Shea, who spoke on behalf of the agreement made with the London employers. When he had finished, I spoke. The meeting was keenly attentive, with many questions. Finally, the call for support was put to the vote and the majority decision was for strike action. They did strike, but unfortunately only for four days, returning to work on the sectarian grounds that their sector was not affected by the clauses affecting the Continuity Rule— though I had warned them in my speech that in 1968 the greater part of London dock was due to be closed down.

Once again we were back to Square One, Sectors 4 and 5 fighting a lone battle, approximately 8,000 men challenging the attack of the Government and the employers (assisted by certain trade union officials of the London Docks' Trade group) on the protective practices we had achieved through years of bitter struggle from 1889 onwards. We were like the little Dutch boy in the folk tale, trying to hold back the sea with one finger in the dyke.

Meanwhile our Northern brothers on the Merseyside were one solid block, 12,000 of them out to a man, determined there would be no return to work until their justifiable demands had been met; at each mass meeting in the Liverpool Sports Stadium, the officials' promises to negotiate if the men would return to work were howled down. No compromise! All or none! We'll stay out for ever! In face of such determination there was a shifting of ground among the Liverpool employers and the Transport & General Workers' Union. Victory was in sight.

Here in London, the Liaison Committee had appointed me to seek an interview at Transport House with our General Secretary, Frank Cousins, who had broken his visit to the United States to return and sort out the London and Liverpool problems. I went alone, because we did not want to embarrass the General Secretary by making it seem like a demand that he recognise the Liaison Committee. My task was to discuss the issue and inform him of our objections, and their reasons. (It has always been my firm opinion that on matters relating to the port industry, particularly in London, he was either ill-informed or misinformed). We hoped to arrive at a formula that would be acceptable to the men and bring about a return to work based on trustworthy assurances that our justifiable grievances would be met.

In order not to take Frank away from other important committees, I arrived at Transport House at 8 a.m., knowing that the General Secretary usually arrived at 9 a.m. But this was one morning when Frank broke his usual custom, and it was 10 o'clock when I was finally ushered into his office. He gave me a very warm welcome, in the presence of the National Docks' Secretary, T. O'Leary, O.B.E. I explained the reason for my visit and outlined the request of the London Liaison Committee. After a patient hearing and many searching questions, with viewpoints also expressed by the National Docks' Secretary, the two of them drew up a formula for the setting up of an enquiry after an immediate return to work. When it was read to me my stomach took on a sinking feeling. It was a negative formula, leaving everything *status quo*. I informed them that I would take it back to the Liaison Committee, but warned that I had no hope of its acceptance.

When I reported back to my Committee, my assessment was confirmed. After taking about fifteen minutes to analyse the formula and sum it up, the Committee decided that they could not accept it as a basis for resumption of work but that we were in duty bound to read it out at the mass meeting convened for the following morning. This should be done, we decided, without recommendation one way or another.

The news of the Liverpool victory had come through, thanks to the very positive help given by Jack Jones, then Assistant General Secretary of our union. The men's determination to have parity with their London brothers on piecework rates had won—and rightly, for after all, a hold full of 2 cwt. bags of sugar weighs just as much in Liverpool as it does in London, the same accident hazards exist on a ten-hour shift. From now on, we felt sure, the northern employers would find it much more difficult to maintain Liverpool as a cheap-labour port.

At 10 a.m. on a bright mid-October morning we opened the meeting. We were about to enter our seventh week of struggle. Overnight, the evening press had made much of my visit to Transport House, and stated that I had come away with a formula to be recommended to the mass meeting. It was one of the most densely-packed gatherings since the beginning of the struggle—about 7,000 men, a battery of reporters, cameramen of the B.B.C. and I.T.V., journalists from Europe, and also a Spanish broadcasting company; not to mention the usual number of Metropolitan and Port of London police, the former standing around me because of the anonymous threats to my person.

Ernie Rice spelled out the recommendations from the General Secretary and the National Docks' Group secretary in his very deliberate and careful manner. As the negative aspects of the report became clear, the atmosphere grew tense with feelings of frustration, anger and disgust. Amidst cries of "No return!" "Negotiate now! Are we less than our Liverpool brothers?" "Out! Out!" Ernie stepped down. Danny Lyons took his place, outlining the gravity of the situation, very ably pointing out the threat that "containerisation" would mean to the National Register in terms of manning; the employers, he said, would never rest until there was a reduction in the London labour force. Then he too stepped down.

The time had come for the moment of truth, and it was my job as Chairman to discover the answer. I was now back on the rostrum—the old, time-worn kitchen chair that has stood my ten-stone weight through countless meetings over the years, starting in 1958 with a few hundred listeners but rising to thousands as confidence and respect built up for the London Liaison Committee, giving it the status of an unofficial shop stewards' committee. And now, in 1967, the schism that had been in existence since 1956 was healed: standing shoulder to shoulder, six weeks without wages or strike pay, stood dockers, stevedores, clerks, young, middle-aged and on the threshold of retirement, one solid mass of 7,000 men, united as a single whole in defence of the protective practices of their trade—torn from the employers in a century of struggle and privation.

As I looked at the sea of faces I could feel myself filling up with emotion. There were the countless men with whom I have worked, sharing good times and bad according to the fluctuations of the shipping trade. Men hardened and toughened by the nature of their work, in an industry that still has one foot back in Dickensian times, ten hours of piecework at breakneck speed, with an accident rate of one man in 1,500 killed, one in eight seriously injured every year and every man averaging four attendances a year for medical treatment; forced to work overtime because of the low basic wage and piecework rates (rates so low that their yield is very little more than the basic hourly rate; a forty-hour week agreement was made in 1964 but it hasn't been operated because the men can't *afford* it). Out there I can see Frankie, who returned to work just three weeks before the strike after a very long and painful illness which entailed the removal of one eye; standing behind him is Roy, a former secretary of the Liaison Committee, young and always bubbling with laughter and sentiment—till Nature pulled him up sharp with a heart attack; he too (married, with three kids) had returned to work only a month before the strike. Beside him is a lovable old character always known as "Shopping-bag" because after a day's work he would always be seen carrying one. Over there on the left is Terry, a clerk, sixty-seven years of age, about to retire, and proud that throughout his fifty years in the industry he has never scabbed.

It was like looking at history. Here in the decades of the past these men's fathers and grandfathers had stood, poorly clad, hungry, but defiant, listening to those great dock fighters and orators of the past who, without the assistance of the modern sound-equipment we enjoy today, shouted themselves hoarse so as to be heard about the noise of the horse-drawn traffic trundling over cobblestones. But those men, their hearers, knew that when

they came to raise their hands for strike action they would be faced
—not with falling behind with their hire-purchase payments, but
with going without food, going home to face their wives and large
broods of children knowing that within a couple of days the cup-
board would be bare, and they'd have to go to the callous relieving officers and the Board of Guardians. Yet if the strikers of 1967
do not face outright want, if the staff of the Social Security appa-
ratus is more human in its approach, it is the *result* of the struggles
of those that went before.

It was my duty as Chairman to put the Liaison Committee's
recommendation to the meeting. I read it out, simple and direct:
"We, the Liaison Committee, cannot accept the recommendation of the General Secretary and National Docks' Labour Group
Secretary as a basis for returning to work. Therefore we ask for
the continuance of the struggle. All those in favour, raise your
hands."

A forest of hands shot up. There were no side-glances. With
only twelve votes against and five abstentions, it was almost unanimous. I carried out our custom and practice by calling one
of the abstainers to come to the restrum and record the vote.
The recommendation was read once more, and again the call
for a vote. The abstainer judged for himself and declared the
result to the meeting.

So there we were, about to enter the seventh week of our
strike, with the employers, the Government, the national press
and the National Docks' Group Committee against us; 7,000
men on a register of approximately 21,000 London port-workers.
If ever there was a time to "stiffen the sinews, summon up the
blood", it was now. The Liaison Committee decided once more
to approach the Establishment, to march once again to the
Minister of Labour and the Prime Minister. But we met with the
usual greeting: sorry, they're not in residence. They'd have been
at home all right if we'd been City bankers. However, as a result
of our pressure through the trade union branches, a precedent
was created; for the first time in the history of the post-war dock
struggles, an unofficial committee was invited to meet the
London Docks' Group Committee (employers' representatives
and trade union officials)! They must have grudged us the privilege, because on the night of the meeting we were kept kicking our
heels in a downstairs hall for almost an hour, and when we did
meet them, with the London and National Docks' Group sec-

retaries in attendance, the atmosphere was cool. After discussion and questions, sometimes heated, a fresh formula was agreed on in order to obtain a return to work. But to the dismay of the Liaison Committee, we learned that when this had been put to the employers they had decided to change the wording of one of the points. Where we had accepted: "That at the 3 a.m. Sector meetings men will be placed into non-continuity work when being transferred between companies", they wanted to make it "men will, *where practical* . . ." which in our opinion negated what we had agreed on. So there we were, back to Square One, and yet only a few words from a return to work.

It was at this stage that I was invited to visit the Universities of Stranraer, Glasgow and Edinburgh, to take part in a teach-in. I went by aeroplane, but owing to poor visibility we arrived at Stranraer thirty minutes behind schedule. I was met by the organising Secretary of the Students' Union, who warned me to expect a lively reception from the students, who unaware of the reason for my late arrival. were riled and impatient. He explained that some of them, if they wanted to hear me out and ask questions, would have to miss lectures and classes, and said I should expect some hostility from rival factions of political societies.

How right he was! As I stepped from the taxi, I was greeted with whistles, hissing, boos and cheers; the lecture hall was packed with about 500 students, boys and girls, and as I went in there was a great crescendo of boos, cheers, hisses, hand-clapping and stamping feet.

It was the stormiest meeting I have ever experienced. But I was determined to keep an even keel and not lose my temper or give way. The University Labour Club had spent a lot of money and time organising this event and as far as I was concerned, I wanted to see they got value for it. The Chairman rose to announce me and explain the reason for my late arrival, but had great difficulty in making himself heard. Having finished the introduction, he sat down. The floor was mine. During my opening remarks the protests of the opposition grew louder and stronger. I thought of Kipling: "If you can keep your head when all about you are losing theirs . . ." and exchanged, without getting angry, some humorous remarks with the interruptors. Gradually I won their respect, if not their agreement, and throughout the remaining ninety minutes of my speech there was respectful silence, except for applause at certain points; and my closing remarks received a standing ovation. I answered questions and commented on points made in the discussion. I left Stranraer for Edinburgh richer in experience, feeling that I had reached a new maturity in public speaking and was steeled against further stormy meetings. Thank you, students of Stranraer!

My visit to Edinburgh was of a much more peaceful character. I found the students very attentive, and very searching in their questions. Afterwards, I gave a question-and-answer interview to the students' newspaper. Here is a verbatim report of it:

STUDENT: Are you opposed the basic idea of decasualisation?

DASH: We are not opposed to decasualisation but to its terms of reference. We find that within the terms of reference there are too many points in favour of employers rather than the men.

STUDENT: Do you think you will succeed in your immediate aims with this strike?

DASH: When the men are determined to smash Tory policies then nothing can stop them. Finally, the Unions and the employers will have to sit down and negotiate. We've done all we can as an unofficial movement. We've bent over backwards to get a solution. We've been three times to Wilson, to Cousins and to the Unholy Trinity, Gunter, who received me very discourteously.

Now it's up to the attendant industries who are directly affected by the strike; we want to get back to work as soon as possible but no one wants to go back to the situation we were in before.

For instance people such as the car workers who are going on short time because the exports are held up; it is up to these industries to put pressure on the government and the employers to make the very small move required to get the men back to work. We are only words away from a solution.

STUDENT: Do you think there will be a backlash against you personally as the economic situation gets worse?

DASH: It seems to me and a lot of the lads that there's a vendetta against the Liaison Committee using this as an excuse. They seem to be scared of losing face. We've done all we can. In fact, we've gone along with the original trade union resolution all the way through the strike. It's the unions who have broken faith with the men and allowed themselves to be intimidated by the Government and the employers.

STUDENT: Do you then feel bitter about the role of the Unions?

DASH: I'm a union member, and although I don't feel they've done enough, I would stress that we're not opposing the unions as such but the employers, the architects of all this. Therefore, we find ourselves in conflict with the National Docks' Group but not the T.G.W.U. Executive.

STUDENT: It is said that one of the main reasons for Britain's economic weakness is the recent series of dock strikes. Do you think this is true and do you think it's fair?

DASH: This is absolute rubbish. When you look at the vast bill for obsolete armaments and the money that's invested in cheap labour overseas in direct competition with the British worker, then you see some of the main causes of our economic weakness. The employers could quite easily meet our demands and have plenty left out of their profits.

STUDENT: Are you a wrecker?

DASH: I don't consider myself a wrecker in any way. Take a look at the injury figures for the docks and the various impositions of the employers and you'll see who's doing the wrecking. This job would wreck anyone. Who are these people to moralise?

STUDENT: It has been suggested that you are a Luddite, implacably opposed to mechanisation.

DASH: I'm not opposed to mechanisation as such. I am opposed to mechanisation when it puts men on the dole. Progress measured by the degree of automation you can get without considering the plight of the displaced worker is not progress at all.

On Ray Gunter and the Red Plot

DASH: I think Ray Gunter ought to see a head shrinker. You know, I feel very sorry for him because I remember a famous American Senator, Forrestal, who got so caught up with this "Red Bug" that his mind became unbalanced and he jumped out of a skyscraper window shouting "There's Reds under the bed!"

M

I should hate to think of Gunter, every time he goes to bed, looking underneath to see if I'm there. I'd much prefer he found a little darling under there.

On Harold Wilson

DASH: I've just been reading the thoughts of Harold Wilson. When he was in opposition he warned the Tories to be careful not to call everyone who criticised their arms programme a Red Plotter. This applies to his management of the economy. That bloke can do an about turn faster than the sentry outside Buckingham Palace. He may not be any good at putting up space rockets, but he's second to none in putting up prices.

On Frank Cousins

DASH: I disagree with him most of the time, but I've got great respect for him because name me another Union leader who'd give up a £9,000 a year government job on a matter of principle?

STUDENT: Do you think the port workers have suffered because the docks haven't been nationalised?

DASH: Certainly. If our industry had been nationalised in the Socialist manner I have outlined we would not be in the present position. We would also be able to serve the country more efficiently.

STUDENT: You have said that you envisage Nationalisation as a form of workers' control, in contrast to the ideas of the present Government. Do you think that even their form of nationalisation would help?

DASH: Any attempt to get employers off our backs, and I hate the employers, would be a step in the right direction. I know from experience that our employers are the most cunning in the world. Of course, there would still be problems under nationalisation. We'd still have problems under Communism. All I'm saying is that they'd be a lot simpler because we'd be dealing with ourselves, the owners of the industry, rather than with private enterprise.

STUDENT: What do you think of the students of this country?

DASH: They're vastly different from the students when I was a young man. Then, in the 1926 strike, it was the students who were doing the blacklegging and the scabbing. That would not happen with today's students. The students today are in the forefront of the international movements against war and social injustice.

I say this sadly because they are leading the industrial workers of this country in these matters, whereas it should be the industrial workers who take the lead in protests against the war in Vietnam, and so on.

I'm not trying to curry favour with you or anything, but whenever you see a demonstration or a protest it is a fact that the students are always in the majority. This is a matter of shame to us in the labour movement.

One thing I like about the students: they never try to be intellectual snobs with me.

STUDENT: What's your attitude on students doing vacation jobs in industry?

DASH: This is of course a political issue. I would say it would be far better for them to concentrate on getting bigger grants than to take part-time jobs from people who have to earn their living in industry.

STUDENT: What do you think about the rise in Overseas Students' fees and aid to overseas-students in general?

DASH: I deplore the rise and I support every progressive step you've taken to make sure it does as little harm as possible. We support any move to get more overseas lads here to study and I only wish we could give you more industrial support.

22

Back to Work

We were now in our eighth week of struggle, with no sign of a breakthrough. The National Docks' Group were adamant, and would not revert to the original wording of the recommendation we had agreed on. One day, when I arrived home from a committee meeting, Ellen told me that the producer of the David Frost programme had telephoned to enquire whether I would be willing to appear on his programme. He had left a message to say he would call on me that evening. This he did. I invited him in to discuss his proposals and right at the start I told him that it was the policy of the Liaison Committee that none of its members would appear on sound ratio or television together with a trade union official, paid or unpaid. It wasn't that we were afraid to face them, but we had continually emphasised that our fight was against the employers, not the trade unions; therefore, if we were to appear on a programme with trade union officials on the set it might appear to the public that we were opposed to them. I was assured that there would be no trade union official in attendance. I next asked if I would be presented as a member of the Communist Party or as Chairman of the Docks' Liaison Committee, and was told, the latter. With these assurances I agreed to appear, expecting that I would be confronted with an employer. It was fixed that the proffered fee should be paid to the London Liaison Committee (it has always been my practice that fees of this kind, paid during disputes, should go to the Committee funds). Before he left, the producer asked permission for his photographer to take a picture of the dockland panorama from my sixteenth-floor window, to be used as a backdrop for the programme.

The studio car arrived on time, and I left home with two of my friends who wanted the experience of attending a live show. What a show it turned out to be, and how truly was I conned!

We were taken to the artistes' and guests' reception room, where drinks were served from a cocktail bar. Then I was whisked off to the make-up specialists in the powder-room. David Frost was there, also being powdered, and I introduced myself to him and again asked whether I would be interviewed as Chairman of the Liaison Committee or as a member of the Communist Party. I was firmly assured that there would be no mention of Communism during the programme—but millions of viewers know that this pledge was not kept.

We took our places on the set, and as soon as I took a look at the audience I saw a number of lay officials of my Union. Among them was one who had been on the sick list during the whole time we had been on strike—but he'd recovered sufficiently to appear on the telly. Another was a chap who had at one time left the industry during a trade recession; later he had come back to the docks, but had left his own union (which had placed an official ban on weekend overtime) and transferred to the Transport & General Workers' Union, which had no such ban.

As the programme proceeded, the suave David Frost was revealed as a "con man"—at least to me and to those of London's dockers who were watching television that night. Every time I attempted to answer one of the questions or statements put to me by the selected occupants of the two front rows, he would switch to another without once giving time to reply properly—and when I objected to his attitude, he made reference to "the Communist". This was the man who had made his reputation in the very popular anti-Establishment programme *That was the Week that Was*, and here he was behaving as if he were the very Establishment itself. People afterwards asked me why I didn't get angry, why I didn't walk off the set? It seemed, and seems still to me, that the Establishment would have *liked* me to appear as a hot-tempered man who cannot take criticism. Well, another lesson learned!

During the following weekend, our Committee met to reassess the situation, and after many hours of discussion came to the conclusion that we had exhausted all avenues of negotiation and had reached an impasse. We were about three weeks away from Christmas, and, knowing what this meant for family life, we reluctantly decided to recommend a return to work until January 1, 1968, and to consider the next steps then, if there had been no change in the situation that had brought us out on strike. The

Committee members took farewell of one another with heavy hearts; but we were realists, and did not feel able to ask the lads of Sectors 4 and 5 to continue on the altar of sacrifice. It was agreed that I should put the matter to them on the Monday morning.

So we gathered on Monday morning, to open the last meeting of our eight-weeks' strike, to address the men who had withstood all the attacks of the press—never was an industry more maligned in an attempt to turn public sympathy away from an industrial dispute: the whole lot of anti-docker venom had been spat at us, lies, distortions, half-truths, but *never* the truth.* The employers had been prepared to dismiss us if we did not call off the dispute and return to work, but had reluctantly changed their minds on the advice of the trade unions—not because the negotiating unions had a soft spot for the Liaison Committee but because they considered that such an action would inflame the whole Port of London to strike against the sackings. The Government (via the Ministry of Labour) had refused to intervene on our behalf and were preparing, doubtless with the support of the Tory opposition, to use the Emergency Powers Act.

It was the most densely-packed meeting we had seen. The lads were standing shoulder to shoulder; there were crowds of news reporters, a great battery of television and other cameras, an unprecedented concentration of Metropolitan police—and for the first time in the history of dockland, a police-*woman* on duty! At first we of the Committee did not attach any special significance to all this—but we were to discover the reason as the meeting progressed.

On time I got up to start the meeting with my usual opening remarks as Chairman, then made way for Ernie Rice who began to give a careful and capable re-cap of the situation. Meanwhile one of the other members of the Committee drew my attention to an elderly woman who was standing very close to the plat-from, looking rather agitated, and chain-smoking. Someone suggested that she might be from the Economic League, but I thought she was just curious. The next moment, she spoke to me, asking permission to address the men. I told her that this could not be permitted, and anyhow it would have to be a committee decision. Thereupon she accused me of being a liar, saying that when I appeared on the *Frost Programme* I had stated that

* Always excepting the *Morning Star*.

anyone could speak at our meetings. I explained to her that I had been referring to our rank and file members and officials. But she seemed too agitated and excited to be reasoned with.

Meanwhile, Ernie Rice had concluded his speech. I got back onto our kitchen chair and read out the Committee's recommendation for a return to work, amid angry protestations from some of the rank and file, particularly our young stalwarts who had been "blooded" in their first industrial strike. I called for the vote. The show of hands in support of the recommendation, while not overwhelming, carried a large enough majority for a return to work. With deep, almost overwhelming emotion, I closed the meeting and got down.

As I began to answer a question from one of the press reporters, the mystery of the agitated lady was revealed. She rushed over to me and swung a resounding slap on the side of my face—and I leave you to guess if the cameras were in position! Thank goodness, I have enough years of experience to discipline myself. Many of the lads surged toward my assailant, but I told them to let her be. The Police Commissioner asked me if I wished to make a charge of assault against her, but I said no. There was a crowd of lads shouting and gesticulating around the woman, who had been joined by a docker whom I recognised—we had been friends for years and he had stood as a Liberal candidate in the recent Council elections. I still had not connected him with the woman who had hit me, but he made an appeal and an apology to me; I discovered that she was his wife. He dissociated himself from her action and said he had warned her to stay away from the meeting when he had learned her intentions. He said his wife was also a member of the Liberal Party: she was liberal all right, specially with that right hand!

Well she achieved plenty of publicity. She was adopted as the heroine of the national press, in particular of the *Daily Mirror* (which suggested that in the New Year's Honours List she should be given the O.B.E.).

Not satisfied with the amount of photographs they had taken at the meeting, the newshounds of the *Mirror* group tailed me home, and took further pictures of me as I got out of my friend's car. Still not satisfied, they hung around the block of flats I live in, until they espied me coming from the lift with two bags of washing, doing a simple homely chore for my wife as most husbands are prepared to do. They followed, taking photo-

graphs, and then went into the laundry shop and asked questions
of the manageress.

I was rather pleased the next day to hear Malcolm Muggeridge,
in the radio programme *Any Questions?*, say that in his opinion the
face-slapping incident was an arranged job. He said it was like
a movie-shot—the crowd scene, all the cameras focused, "Action!
Take One—" and the principal character walks over and slaps.
He went on to speak about an incident that happened when he
was in Berlin and there was a supposed *"escapee"* about to jump
from the East side of the Wall into the West; the press photographers had got him to jump several times so that they could
take satisfactory pictures. I think the fact of the policewoman
being in attendance supports this view.

Looking back in time, and evaluating our nine-weeks' struggle,
I consider that the strike was not lost. We lost wages, true. But
our gain was that the employers were now fully aware that we
were not tame mice and that we would not stand for any kind of
intimidation. From the time of our return, they took every precaution to avoid misusing the clauses concerning the Continuity
Rule that had caused the struggle. We had restored to the negotiating committees of our accredited trade unions some of their
long-lost militancy and as a result the £17 0s. 0d. minimum was
agreed by the Ministry of Labour. A closer unity had been
achieved between man and man, and the relationship between
the rank and file and the paid officials of the trade union was far
friendlier. The setting up of an official shop stewards' movement,
as recommended in the Devlin Report, was about to begin.

Christmas being over, the local trade unions made preparation
for the convening of mass meetings for the election of a shop
stewards' committee for each individual firm of employers. The
first meeting, held in a Port of London Authority works canteen,
was that of the men of the Thames 65 Company. The acting
Senior Divisional Officer (full-time) of the union, Brother Bill
Munday, had the unpleasant job of reading out to the meeting
the constitutional ruling of the Transport & General Workers'
Union which states that members of the Communist Party cannot,
hold office either paid or unpaid. Immediately he mentioned this
rule there was an uproar and shouts of "No politics! Providing
he is a docker and a fully paid-up member of his union, White or

Blue, we'll nominate whom we choose!" Several men got up to leave but the Chairman, Vicky Turner, for whom the men have a deep respect, appealed to them to remain and keep calm. This they did and eventually it was accepted that since it was a joint meeting, the Constitution of the Transport & General Workers' Union could not be binding of the members of the National Amalgamated Stevedores' & dockers' Union, who could nominate one of ours if they so wished; the ruling would have to be set aside.

Order was restored, and the election took place. Ernie Rice, member of the Liaison Committee, Transport & General Workers' Union, Communist, was nominated and received the highest vote. Young Micky Fenn, Member of the Liaison Committee, National Amalagamated Stevedores' & Dockers' Union, Communist, was nominated and elected.

The next day, at the meeting convened for Scrutton & Maltby's, with 1,950 men in attendance, Vicky Turner former member of the Liaison Committee received the highest vote; David Timothy, member of the Liaison Committee, National Amalgamated Stevedores' & Dockers' Union, Communist, was elected; Buck Baker, former member of the Liaison Committee, Transport & General Workers' Union, Communist, was elected; and I, Chairman of the Liaison Committee, member of the Transport & General Workers' Union, and a Communist, received the second highest vote.

At the Southern Stevedores' meeting Ted Kirby, Transport & General Workers' Union, Communist, was elected with the highest vote. For the Port of London Authority Danny Lyons, Transport & General Workers' Union, Communist, was elected.

Thus within a week, five members of the Liaison Committee, all Communists, were elected and endorsed by the men as their shop stewards. The London Docks' Group Committee of the Transport & General Workers' Union could not swallow this, however. The non-Communist stewards thereupon refused to sign the statutory form declaring that they were not members of the Communist Party. The Docks' Group Committee refused to issue credentials. The "Blue" union, (National Amalgamated Stevedores' & Dockers') had no such ban; their members enjoyed democratic rights; so their elected stewards were issued with credentials and these were given full recognition by the Port employers.

The London Docks' Group continued its refusal to accept us, and called in the Regional Officer and the London Docks' Group Officer to address the shop-stewards-elect, which they did, putting great stress on the constitution of the union, which rules that an official must sign a form stating that he is not a member of a "proscribed" organisation. It was pointed out to them that on Merseyside, credentials had been given to members of the Communist Party who were now acting as shop stewards, and that Communists had been acting as shop stewards in many trade groups of the Union. To their great credit, the non-Communist stewards again refused to sign.

What an undemocratic rule for the trade union to have! It denies the right of a fully-paid-up member to nominate and elect a fellow member of his choice to a lay or full-time office; it denies the right of full participation to a member who happens to be a member of the Communist Party of Great Britain; and if a non-Communist decides, through political experience, to join the Communist Party, then he must declare this and relinquish his post.

The London Docks' Group made one further attempt to remove the Communists but were again rebuffed by the non-Communist stewards. In the meantime, the Executive Committee of the Transport & General Workers' Union, at a specially convened meeting, decided by thirty-two votes to two to recommend support for the removal of the ban at the next Rules Revision Conference to be held in July 1968.*

In January 1968, the Shop Stewards' Committee of the firm of Scrutton & Maltby, to which I had been elected, met with the employers' representatives, the chief superintendent in charge of the labour force in Sector 4 and the top management from the firm's city office, which included a Company Director and a retired Naval Commander. They had invited us to come to an informal introduction meeting. They came to our committee room, after we had finished discussing the terms that would enable us to function efficiently on behalf of the men who had elected us.

Their elected Chairman introduced their side. Our Chairman, Vicky Turner, introduced each of us. Cordial handshakes all

---

I finished writing my story before that date, but am happy to say that the conference removed the 18-year-old ban on Communists, restoring full democratic rights to all members.

round. Then their spokesman said a few words: how pleased they were to meet us, and how very important it was for both sides of the industry that the Shop Stewards' Committee should succeed and how both sides should co-operate in team-work because Messrs Scruttons have always been concerned about the welfare of their employees. (I thought to myself, what a lot of con! It was during the second week of our recently-concluded strike that they'd sent out circulars to each of their employees threatening them with the sack unless there was a return to work.) Then there were more short speeches from both sides. In my own contribution I ventured to say that any agreements we reached would only be provisional, because within two and a half years "we'll be nicking the lot from you—that's of course if Harold Wilson doesn't do another about-turn—and by that I mean nationalisation!" This caused chuckles from our side. The meeting ended with cordial assurances from the employers that everything would be done to smooth out the problems.

As I bring my story to an end (April 1968) we have been making great efforts to get the shop stewards' system functioning in Sector 4. We even compromised on our first demand for what we considered the necessary procedure to enable us to work. But the employers don't seem willing to co-operate even on our compromise. We rather think they don't want a shop stewards' committee after all—perhaps because there are too many Communists and former members of the Liaison Committee. At the moment of writing, we have informed the employers of the Royal Group of Docks that we have done all we possibly can, even to the point of compromise, to get the shop stewards' committee functioning. But if they want it all on the cheap we say to them: "Thus far and no further". We can revert to the *status quo ante*. The Liaison Committee has not been wound up; it's only been put in cold storage.

23

Concluding

I was just coming to the end of my autobiography when I was asked by a producer of the B.B.C. Television Studio at Shepherds Bush, London, if I would be prepared to take part in a new satirical programme called *The Eleventh Hour*. The idea was for me to read my own Obituary—written by myself. It was a new experience for me, and I rather fancied the oddity of sitting on a "live" programme and reading about my "dead" self. Here is what I said:

"Mr Jack Dash, who died last week when trying to pacify a mob of re-deployed port employers, was the first Communist Minister of Labour in the Bertrand Russell Coalition Government of 1971. His term of office was marked by the implementation of the Harold Wilson-Ray Gunter Award scheme for the most promising ex-company-director recruited to the shop floor in memory of two of the most militant employers' leaders. He also launched the 'Free Sea Travel for Dockers' system.

"Mr Dash became politically active at an early age, and in 1936 he joined the Communist Party and remained a member until his death. In 1937, he was awarded the Tolpuddle Martyrs' Medal for trade union recruiting. In 1945, Mr Dash decided to become a docker, and he was accordingly recommended to a place in the industry by the Port Employers' Federation. It is understood that a number of the Federation's members decided later that this may have been a mistake. From the start of his working life, Jack Dash was an industrial militant, and he once said that the only epitaph he wanted was:

> Here lies Jack Dash
> All he wanted was
> To **separate** them from their cash

(This is thought to have been one of his frequent friendly references to the dock employers, with whom he had a close, lifelong relationship based on a warm mutual dislike.) For a number of reasons, the employers considered that Mr Dash was a bad influence on the dock industry, and they alleged that he had led a number of unofficial strikes which had a disastrous effect on their profits. When Mr Dash pointed out that these strikes had helped to raise the minimum wages in the docks from £9 in 1959 to £17 in 1967 and £30 in 1972, the employers replied that this was exactly what they were complaining about.

"Long before he joined the Government, Jack Dash was a public figure. For this he had to thank the national newspapers, and throughout his life he felt a proper sense of gratitude to Fleet Street for the painstaking and sympathetic approach which marked all their dealings with him. Mr Dash particularly appreciated the Press Council's censure of the *Daily Express*, printed by that paper after the Devlin Report in 1965, and the annual series of apologies printed in the *Daily Telegraph* after every third story they wrote about him. However, Mr Dash's favourite newspaper, after the *Morning Star*, was the *Daily Mirror*. The *Mirror* could always be relied on to maintain his position as a controversial figure and keep his post-bag full of rather short anonymous letters. The *Mirror* was also remarkable for its scrupulous use of its uniquely influential position and its respect for Mr Dash's private life. It is thought that when he described the *Daily Mirror* as 'the navvies' comic' Mr Dash was being humorous."

I thank you dear reader, if you have read so far, for your interest and patience. May I offer a bit of advice, especially to the young? Read and learn the history of the British labour movement, the working class, its struggles and development, its twin creations, the trade unions and the Co-operative Movement, from which has developed the finest principle of humanism, international brotherhood. And let us continue the struggle of the pioneers of our great movement for a socialist Britain where the people will be the rightful owners of the land and the means of production; for the ending of class privilege; for equal opportunities for education, leisure, social services free to all regardless of race, religion or colour. For human dignity, the right of every single being.

Ah Love! could thou and I with fate conspire
To grasp this sorry Scheme of Things entire,
Would we not shatter it to bits—and then
Re-mould it nearer to the Heart's Desire!